Over 30 Years on the Road
to Memories, Music
& Legend

An AMERICAN Journey

Joseph S. Bonsall

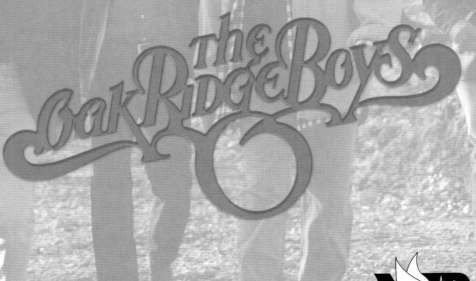

New Leaf Press

AN AMERICAN JOURNEY

First Printing: October 2004

Cover by Janell Robertson, Green Forest, AR
Interior design by Brent Spurlock
Cover photo (front, back left): David Johnson

ISBN: 0-89221-601-8
Library of Congress Catalog Number: 2004112801

New Leaf Press

Dedicated to our wives:

Brenda, Donna, Mary Ann, and Norah Lee

TABLE OF CONTENTS

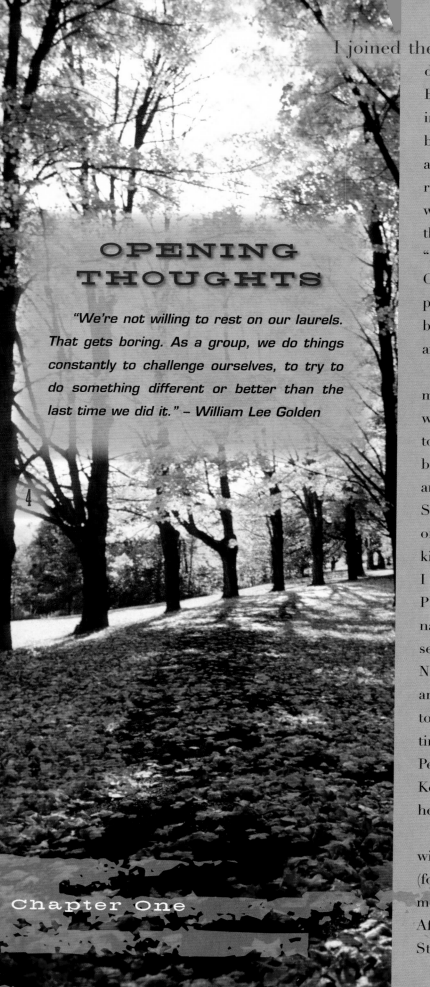

"We're not willing to rest on our laurels. That gets boring. As a group, we do things constantly to challenge ourselves, to try to do something different or better than the last time we did it." – William Lee Golden

4

Chapter One

I joined the Oak Ridge Boys in October, 1973 at the tender age of 25 years old. I was living in a suburb of Buffalo, New York at that time and I had been singing with and managing a young cutting edge Gospel band called the Keystones. I had been struggling along for six years and it seemed like the time was right for a major change in my life. My young wife was pregnant and, although I was having fun with this little group, we were starving to death and just "not making ends meet" as my mother used to say. Our young bass singer, Richard Sterban, had been a part of the Keystones for several years as well, and he basically faced the same problem. Three young sons and a wife at home with an empty refrigerator.

Richard left the Keystones at the end of 1970, moved to Nashville, Tennessee, and took a job singing with J. D. Sumner and the Stamps Quartet. I hated to see him go because, not only was he my absolute best friend on the planet, but he was a wonderful and unique talent. The guy could flat out sing bass. Such a natural low tone and timber to his voice. Not only that, he was always a levelheaded and honest kind of guy that you could really count on in a pinch. I had known Richard since I was in high school in Philadelphia and he was a young bass singer wannabe from Camden, New Jersey. Back then, he was selling men's clothes at Gimbels department store in Northeast Philly, and I would go up there, follow him around, and talk Gospel quartets while he was trying to sell some guy a pair of Chinos. He performed part-time with The Eastman Quartet out of Lansdale, Pennsylvania, and eventually went full-time with the Keystone Quartet (the Keystones), a group that he helped to originate.

When I was just 19, Richard hired me to sing with the Keystones. We moved the group to Buffalo (for some reason that I can't remember) and for the most part, we have been singing together ever since. After the Keystones, Richard's journey with the Stamps Quartet would lead him on a tour singing

backup with "the King," Elvis Presley, and eventually taking a job singing bass with the Oak Ridge Boys in October of 1972.

How I managed to end up singing again with Richard, along with Duane Allen and William Lee Golden, is quite a story. One could never have imagined such a scenario. Here was my long-time friend singing with Elvis and then joining up with my all time favorite Gospel quartet, the mighty Oak Ridge Boys. It so happened that throughout 1970, 1971 and 1972, my little Keystone group promoted Gospel concerts all over New York state. We would bring major Gospel acts up from the south and put on shows in towns like Jamestown, Elmira, Buffalo, Rochester, and even on down to Erie and Corry, Pennsylvania. My favorite group to promote was the Oak Ridge Boys. I dearly loved those guys for many reasons.

Richard (second from left) as part of the Stamps Quartet, touring with Elvis, early 1970s.

The Keystones in 1973. Joe is on the far right in the second row.

First of all, they were the most innovative group in all of Gospel music. From a creative standpoint, they feared absolutely nothing. They wore their hair longer and were much more fashion minded than any of the other cookie cutter quartets, who all dressed alike right down to their shoe tops. Most of these groups still performed live with just a piano player (the old fashioned way), but the Oaks were the first Southern Gospel group to hire a complete band with a full-fledged, hippy looking rock and roll drummer, and they certainly weren't afraid to stretch the boundaries of their music.

They had won a truckload of awards for their albums, *Light*; *Talk About The Good Times*; and *Thanks*, which featured some songs written by a contemporary Christian black man by the name of Andre Crouch, as well as many rock and country-flavored songs. The Oak Ridge Boys were taking Gospel music to an entirely new and exciting level, and I was a huge fan. These guys were just so very cool. You must realize that this was the early seventies and, unlike the Christian and Gospel music of today which has a wide and varied commercial appeal from country sounds to urban rap, folks back then were just not as open minded to a Gospel group that believed the music of Jesus should have just as much creativity and soul as any other kind of music. I certainly agreed and bought into the entire philosophy. Therefore, the Keystones

also took on an Oaks' attitude with our look as well as our sound. It was fun and we won a lot of kids to Christ with our dedication and music appeal, just as the Oaks were doing on a much larger scale.

When Richard left the Keystones, I tried out many bass singers to fill his slot and the mission was impossible. Nobody could sing like "Ol' Stretch" (a nickname given to him because the guy really knew how to stretch a dollar), so to be more like the Oak Ridge Boys, I hired a bunch of rock musicians.

During this time period, I became very good friends with the Oaks. William Lee Golden and I would talk on the phone at length, and he would share his philosophies and visions and dreams with me. I would talk to him from my little rented apartment in Kenmore, New York, and when I would hang up the phone I would feel energized, because here was a man who was always ready to do whatever it took to make a viable mark in the music business, and I gleaned a lot of knowledge from him. We also worked out some dates wherein the Oaks would come north, and Golden would reciprocate by bringing the Keystones south on more than one occasion. I thought the guy hung the moon and stars, and I am still not sure that he didn't hang a few of them.

Perhaps the most reliable and consistent singer I had ever heard was the Oaks' lead singer, Duane Allen, and I am proud and honored to also call him a friend. Duane, as well as William, believed in what I was doing up North and felt like the Keystones were a viable act. Duane built a studio in his basement and started a record label called Superior Records. He invited my group to his home in Hendersonville, Tennessee, on many occasions to record new music. He produced about ten albums for the Keystones, which not only provided some good product to sell but constantly kept us growing and looking forward from a musical standpoint.

Duane would say, "You must constantly keep the music fresh. New material will keep you excited about what you are doing. Always record quality songs, for that is the most important thing that you can do. Your show will be better and people won't get tired of you. Remember, the great song is the key."

Duane still lives by that very same sound philosophy today, and the Oaks have hung their hat on that peg for decades. Yes, these were great times for a young and aspiring singer and it was the influence of the man we call "the Ace" who constantly inspired me to keep on going and to never give up on my dreams. Duane Allen was, and is to this very day, a hero to me.

When Oaks' bass singer Noel Fox left the road in 1972, William Lee Golden called Richard Sterban. Richard nearly jumped through the phone and was so excited about the opportunity to sing with the Oak Ridge Boys. They immediately recorded an album called *Street Gospel*, which would become a classic example of the Oaks' ever-evolving and revolutionary style of music in the early 70s.

9

The Oaks with Minnie Pearl, Roy Acuff, and Grandpa Jones

So, the pieces were starting to fall into place. My best friend was now singing with the Oak Ridge Boys and, in so doing, he was also singing with two other men who had grown to mean so much to me on a personal and professional level. Just one year later, the Oaks' long-time and very popular tenor, Willie Wynn, left the group.

William Lee Golden called me. He told me that he and Duane believed in my talent and loved my energy and in their minds, I was the only one who could fit in with the Oaks at this time. He called me the missing piece of the puzzle and said, "Oh by the way, your good friend Richard says to come on down. It's time to sing together again."

Aside from becoming a Christian, the birth of my daughter, my eventual marriage to Mary, and the death of my precious mother, this phone call from William Lee Golden on a beautiful October evening in 1973 was one of the biggest life-changing events in my life. I would be moving on down to Hendersonville, Tennessee, and I would become a member of the mighty Oak Ridge Boys. I would be making music with my friends right up until this present day, even as you are reading this book.

It has been a long and winding road, to quote the Beatles, and it has also been an incredible ride. Over all these passing years, the Oak Ridge Boys have become the quintessential American music group. We play over 160 days a year in beautiful theaters, performing arts centers, state and county fairs, private corporate events, first class casino resorts, and huge music festivals all over this great country of ours and beyond. We have earned every award imaginable and our records have topped the music charts for three decades. We have sold in excess of 20 million records, and we are still making new and fresh music each year. Our songs, from "Y'all Come Back Saloon" to "Elvira," "Bobbie Sue," and "Thank God For Kids," have become standards in the world of every genre of music. Our Gospel songs are still loved and appreciated by our audience in whatever the concert venue. God has truly blessed the Oak Ridge Boys and, to a man, we are thankful to Him for His blessings upon us.

I want to thank Tim Dudley and all of our friends at New Leaf Press for the opportunity to share our story throughout the pages of this amazing book. Thanks also to our "godfather" and manager Jim Halsey, as well as Joe Sugarman of BluBlocker Sunglasses for their early support and vision for this project.

I am proud to be able to write the text that appears on the pages ahead. Instead of writing a history as such of the Oaks, I have chosen instead to write about the Oaks in more of an anecdotal way. A memoir or narrative, if you will, containing glimpses into the past as well as the present that will reflect who we are and how we arrived at this point in our lives and careers.

In so doing, perhaps a complete picture will emerge for you the reader as to what the Oak Ridge Boys are really all about. So, take a good hard look at all the pictures, for each one reveals a story in and of itself and, as your author, I will try to add some good stories and reflections that will perhaps place you right there on the tour bus with us.

So climb on aboard the Oak Ridge Boys' *Red, White, and BluBlocker* tour bus.

Your bunk is ready. Hang your clothes in the closet and throw your travel bag in a bin underneath.

Golden is brewing some good, bold Starbucks coffee, Duane Allen ("the Ace") is listening to song demos while watching Fox News on the satellite dish. Richard is just waking up, and I am sitting in the back lounge tapping away on my laptop computer while watching "ESPN SportsCenter" on the second dish receiver. Our road manager, Todd Brewer, is on the cell phone talking to a promoter or a motel manager someplace and the very capable Billy Smith, AKA Ralph Kramden, is driving the big MCI coach through Somewhere, USA, on Interstate Anywhere.

"Come on in" and take your coat off. Make yourself right at home. There are plenty of snacks in the drawers and lots of good stuff in the fridge. Diet Vanilla Cokes are in the cooler in the back and there is bottled water in the cooler up front.

No doubt we are on our way to another town to sing for the fine folks who live there. People who have taken their valuable time and spent some of their hard-earned money to gather up as one and listen to the Boys sing their songs.

Duane David Allen, William Lee Golden, Richard Anthony Sterban, and Joseph Sloan Bonsall — "Loving God and Loving Each Other." The story never really ends!

A Mother's Perspective

About the time Richard Sterban graduated from his New Jersey high school, he made the decision to become a professional singer. His mother, Vickie, says that she and Richard's father, Edward, "were happy, however, we wanted Richard to finish college first."

But it was only after one year at Trenton State, where he was studying for a music degree in hopes of becoming a choir director, that Richard received an offer from the Keystones. Because of his enthusiasm, his parents gave their blessing.

Vickie remembers that Richard inherited his bass voice from his father (although Edward was not a singer).

Eventually, the Stamps asked Richard to relocate to Tennessee, and that led to his association with Elvis Presley. A few years later, he provided the bass anchor that would propel the Oak Ridge Boys to superstardom.

Vickie said that her all-time favorite song to hear Richard sing "has got to be a Gospel song," probably "Just a Little Talk with Jesus," and her favorite song that he has recorded with the Oak Ridge Boys is "Dream On."

Richard is a rock. He is steady and sure and you can count on him every moment of every day. How many guys do you know like that? I would guess not many. His dry sense of humor keeps us laughing and his contribution to the group earns our respect daily. Oh, and as I said before, the man can flat out sing bass!

Richard Sterban takes more of a leadership role in our business every year. As mentioned elsewhere in this book, his conservative nature and his even-keeled decision-making has helped the Oak Ridge Boys to enjoy a good balance of keeping a big show on the road, while being very cost-conscious.

Richard fields the majority of the many press interviews that come our way and sometimes will do as many as five phone interviews just to help promote one date. We all do these *phoners*, but Richard usually takes on the lion's share.

His representation of the group on radio and in newspaper articles is always first class as his sheer enthusiasm never wavers. He is also an amateur meteorologist; therefore, we always know what the weather will be like in any given town that we are about to visit.

Richard's intro to the world of music belies his pragmatic nature. The year was 1976, and the Oak Ridge Boys were opening several shows for Freddy Fender. Fender was the Tex-Mex superstar at the time. His unusual voice, coupled with some great songs, like "Before the Next Teardrop Falls," made him a sensation.

We were thrilled to be on part of his tour. These shows provided an opportunity for us to try out some of the new country songs we had just learned, and one night in particular helped pave the way for much needed optimism.

Thousands of people were waiting for Freddy Fender to sing his hits at the Arizona State Coliseum, but first they had to listen to a brand new Gospel (turning country) group called the Oak Ridge Boys. We had worked up a dynamite rendition of the old classic, "Faded Love." Richard sang the verses, and we all came in on the chorus with a full harmony sound. When Richard stepped up to the microphone and began to tenderly sing the first words of the first verse, the huge crowd went absolutely bananas. Girls were screaming and yelling. By the time Richard got to the second verse, the screaming was so loud that no one could hear the last chorus. Richard actually looked bewildered. We kept pointing at him and the girls kept screaming. I knew at that point that we were going to make it big time. After the show, a shaken Richard Sterban apologized to Duane, Golden, and me. He felt that the screaming might have taken away from the group as a whole, and he was sorry for the outburst. We all hugged him and told him to just keep on doing what he was doing and not to worry about it. Is there any doubt why we love this man?

Richard is a part owner of the Nashville Sounds AAA baseball team. He is pictured here with pitching coach and former major leaguer Darold Knowles.

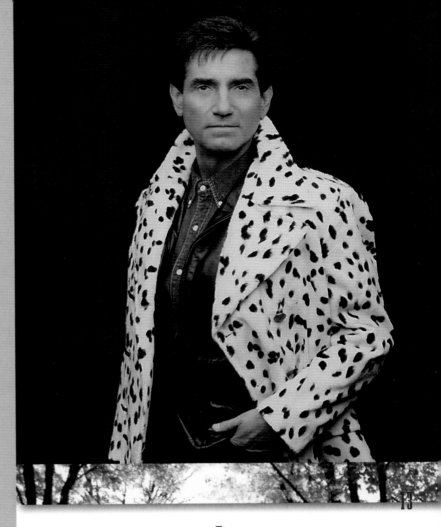

RICHARD'S BOTTOM LINE

THERE IS NO MORE OF A SOLID INDIVIDUAL ON THIS EARTH THAN RICHARD STERBAN; ALWAYS LEVELHEADED, ALWAYS READY TO GO THE EXTRA MILE, AND ALWAYS GIVING EVERY DAY HIS ABSOLUTE BEST. HE IS ALSO MY BEST FRIEND.

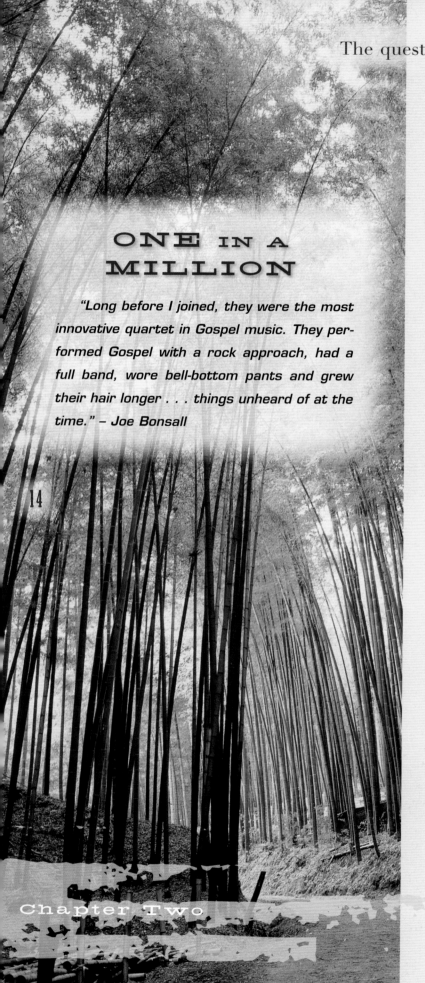

ONE IN A MILLION

"Long before I joined, they were the most innovative quartet in Gospel music. They performed Gospel with a rock approach, had a full band, wore bell-bottom pants and grew their hair longer . . . things unheard of at the time." – Joe Bonsall

14

The question that is most often presented to the Oak Ridge Boys by the media is, "How do you manage to keep on going after all of these years?" Or a variation of such, "Why do you still maintain this kind of pace after all of these years?"

Each Oak always answers the question in pretty much the same way. The actual words may vary a bit, but the bottom line is always, "Hey, we love what we do."

"Well, I guess we are afraid that if we slow down, we just might stop. Therefore, we don't ever slow down."

"We have been able to plan every aspect of our career over all these years. However, we have never been able to formulate a plan on how to stop. To stop being the Oak Ridge Boys is totally unthinkable!"

"Willie Nelson says, 'I sing and I play golf, which one do you want me to stop doing?' Great answer, and we don't even play golf!"

"Our hands are still in the cookie jar here. We sing songs for a living."

Again, bottom line . . . "We love what we do."

This is your answer. Simple and easy as pie, although in reality there is much more to it than that. It takes a lot of hard work to keep a group like the Oaks alive for decades. When you are a group, it is imperative to be constantly pulling together as a team. You must love and respect each other and you must always keep an open mind and heart as to each other's feelings and opinions.

It is not always about you! It is about making the right decisions for the group. It takes common sense, dedication, good business sense, good people around you who know what they are doing, a willingness to sacrifice and to always go that extra mile, while giving each and every song of every show every ounce of energy that you can muster.

Then, it takes a lot of God's blessings, good health, the total support of your family, and a small

dose of old-fashioned luck sprinkled here and there across the years. There also has to be some real talent, genuine charisma, and a healthy dose of magic in the mix, as well. And this group has always possessed all of the above and more.

And did I mention? "You have to *love it! Really love it!*"

I have said many times that you could line up one million guys, keep on picking out four at a time and stand them up behind the microphones. I assure you that you would never, ever, make an "Oak Ridge Boys" out of them. The Oaks are a very unique group of men.

Consider each individual voice. On his own merit, each man can sing with a very unique style. Richard, the obvious, incredible bass, William Lee, the soulful country baritone. Duane, the smooth as silk yet powerful lead. And me, with a tenor voice that really sounds like no one else.

We have all had big hit records with our solo voices out in front. And yet, when all four come together and meld as one, in all honesty, the harmony is amazing. Whether we are singing softly, or whether we are in our big-voiced "power harmony" mode, the blend is surreal.

Each voice has plenty of versatility and range that allows each man to be able to take a lead, while the others can form various harmonies around that lead. A good example of our stock-and-trade sound are songs like "Sail Away" and "Fancy Free": Duane Allen singing the lead note, William on a harmony note below him, and me on the high harmony. (Richard is always anchored down on the lowest note of the chord – that never changes!)

On a song like "Ozark Mountain Jubilee," we switch it all around with the top three voices. William Lee Golden sings the lead notes and Duane sings the harmony below him. I will sing lead on a song like "Love Song" or "Elvira," and Duane will sing up above me. On "I Guess It Never Hurts to Hurt Sometime," I sing the lead on tenor and the others harmonize underneath that lead. This kind of creativity within our very sound structure allows us to utilize a lot of variety in our music.

We can sing any kind of song with any kind of feel just by allowing ourselves the freedom to do so. No matter the genre of the song – Gospel, country, bluegrass, Cajun or rock and roll – the actual sound of the Oaks still never loses its identity. Simply put, no matter how we stack the harmony, audiences have no trouble recognizing the distinct Oaks sound.

The fusion of our different backgrounds, roots, and personalities not only works to make our sound unique, but these very things have molded us into four very distinct individuals as well. Perhaps that alone is one of the major catalysts of our success. Somehow, it all works out.

When William Lee Golden shouts from the stage, "I feel like singin' all night!" he really means it. The show never ends for Golden. He *loves to sing*. To him, each song is important and each song reflects a story that touches someone in that audience. He is a man who enjoys the attention and those folks out there who love him are repaid over and over again for their dedication.

William Lee Golden always gives all of himself to his family, his fans, and his friends. While some of us might crave a bit more privacy, I believe that William would allow everyone that comes to the show to go on home with him and have breakfast!

William Lee is also a man with a clear vision. A man who has been able to turn dreams, seemingly out of reach, into stark reality. There is no other like him anywhere in this solar system. If you ever get to spend time with him, cherish that time.

No one works harder at keeping the Oaks afloat than Duane Allen. He is on a constant, everyday mission to keep things going from a good business standpoint, as well as keeping us fresh in a creative way. He is a tireless song man who knows how to dig for a good piece of material. He is a friend to publishers and songwriters alike. This very unique Nashville music community has learned to trust him over the

The Oak Ridge Boys' Red, White, & BluBlocker bus, 2003.

The Boys with music students at Belmont
University in Nashville.

years with their best songs and the Oaks have been the beneficiaries of his hard work over and over again, throughout our many years of recording.

As much as we all love to sing, we also might have withered on the vine years ago, if not for Duane's constant drive. I am not sure that he even sleeps. In my humble opinion, he is also one of the top three singers in the history of the music business. There is Duane Allen, Randy Owen of Alabama, and Glen Payne of the Cathedral Quartet. He is consistent and true as a human being and consistent and true every night on stage.

There is no more of a solid individual on this earth than Richard Sterban. Always levelheaded, always ready to go the extra mile, and always giving each day his absolute best. The man cares, on a very deep and personal level, about how he presents himself. And that river runs a lot deeper than just wearing the most up-to-date fashions and singing good bass every night. Richard is a *foundation*. He is a *rock*. He is steady and sure, and you can count on him every moment of every day.

In all honesty, I believe that each of the four members of the Oak Ridge Boys was destined to succeed at his chosen field of endeavor because

A sound bite for the evening news.

19

each member has succeeded in becoming a good, solid man. Four guys who all grew up in America believing that if he worked hard, sacrificed, loved God, was honest and trustworthy, and gave each opportunity that presented itself every ounce of energy that he possessed, then good things would surely happen.

Good things have happened, to be sure. The cotton fields of Alabama, the plains of Texas, and the streets of Philadelphia and Camden, New Jersey are a long way from the big time music career of the Oak Ridge Boys but it was growing up in these diverse surroundings with a dream in our hearts and perhaps a star in our pocket that brought us all to this point. No silver spoons on this table. Our parents worked hard and sacrificed much so that we could live out our dreams. They loved us and inspired us, and they constantly reminded us that we could rise up and become anything that we wanted to be. We believed them!

The Oaks are individually diverse, but there are also many common threads woven into the tapestry that holds us together like super glue. In our hearts we are group men. All for one and one for all not only worked for the Three Musketeers, but it has become a way of life for the four Oak Ridge Boys, as well.

We always get an enthusiastic crowd at Fan Fair!

We truly love and respect each other on every level of existence. I wouldn't dare tell you that we always see eye to eye on everything, but our *price-to-earning ratio* is a good one, and our *on-base slugging percentage* definitely leads the league!

We have each managed to stand like mighty oak trees, yet we have also learned to bend and weave with the breeze and each other like willows. I may have a great idea, but someone else may have a better one. Well, hey, let's go with the better one.

The music business is as tough or as easy as you want to make it. You can act like a bunch of prima donnas bathing yourself in self-importance and ego — and literally alienate every promoter, radio manager, song publisher, employee, and fan in your circumference of being, or. . . .

How about this? Keep your perspectives in line and realize that you are *not* the most important being on the planet just because you have achieved success and had your songs played on the radio.

Let's *not* make ridiculous demands. Let's show up, shake hands, smile, be nice to everybody, put on a great show, get the check, board the bus, and head to the next town. It sounds simple because it is, and one good example of the end results is playing the Kentucky State Fair for 30 consecutive years.

This is a wonderful, common thread shared by my partners. And it is certainly one of many good reasons why we are still touring and singing today on a very high level.

That kind of work ethic and people skills, coupled with a rocking stage show, have kept the Oaks alive in our bleakest days, guided us through our biggest career moments, and helped us maintain a very viable career right up to this very moment (in Myrtle Beach, South Carolina, looking at the Atlantic Ocean and pecking away on my laptop computer, while preparing for a show at the Alabama Theater, where we have played over thirty times).

But again, the success of the Oak Ridge Boys still revolves around four men who enjoy singing together. A pure love for the very sound that comes forth when our four voices blend together in perfect harmony. It is a wonderful thing to hear, and it is a blast to be one of those making it happen.

I referred to this sound as "power harmony" earlier, and that just about sums it up. A tenor, a lead, a baritone, and a bass just letting it fly vocally. Singing big! Not necessarily singing hard, but still singing with an edge.

We also call it "singing green." Say the word "greeeeeeennn." Feel the hard *e* sound. That is the edge.

You don't want to sing "bluuuuuuuueeeeee." That is a darker sound. The sound must be green. Alive and vibrant.

Duane Allen refers to it as singing with a smile in your voice. Try it. Put a grumpy look on your face and sing "Amazing Grace." Then, think happy, smile, and sing it again. The difference is extreme, and can even be a deciding factor as to whether or not a song is a hit.

Many times in the studio, a good producer like Ron Chancey or Michael Sykes, or Duane Allen will say, "That was good, now sing it again with a smile in your voice."

I assure you, it is *always* better.

We have had that smile in our voices for a long time, and the end of this road is not visible to us right now. The Oak Ridge Boys just keep on singing year after year. Like magical little Energizer bunnies, we just keep going.

Our famous Hirschfeld caricature commissioned for the Radio City Music Hall performance.

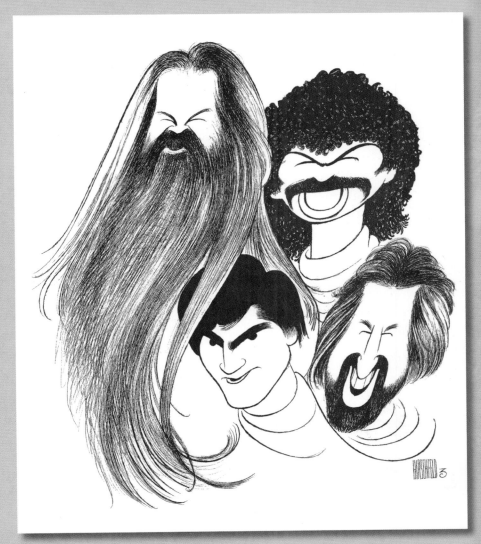

21

I would guess that only bad health could slow us down. God keeps on blessing us though, and for this we are very thankful. The Boys may not be the youngest guys on the corner anymore, but we are still feeling good. Go ahead, book us on a huge festival with a bunch of new and younger acts and you will see that we hold our own quite well. In fact, they had better put on a good pair of singing britches to keep up with us!

We have earned a lot of respect from our peers in the music business, but I've heard some younger acts make remarks like, "I hope that when we get older, we're still not out there on the road like the Oak Ridge Boys."

Or, "Our group is finished singing our hits, they've become boring to us."

Well, the above-mentioned acts don't have to worry about it anymore, because they have ceased to exist.

The long haul is not for everyone. The odds against a long career in the music business are indeed staggering. The long haul exists only for a special and very blessed few. The one in a million!

The Oak Ridge Boys!

THREADS AND BEGINNINGS

The making of the first atomic bomb — and the Oak Ridge Quartet — both exploded onto the world scene in the mid-1940s. The group originated as the Georgia Clodhoppers in Knoxville, Tennessee, near the end of WWII, eventually taking the name of a nearby city, where they often performed at the Oak Ridge nuclear plant. Over the course of the group's history, there have been nearly 50 members to take the stage, first as the Oak Ridge Quartet, then as the Oak Ridge Boys, in the 1960s. The current membership first came together in 1973 — and the rest is history.

24

I talk a lot about "common threads" in this book. The terminology seems to makes a lot of sense as it relates to the Oak Ridge Boys. There are many of these very distinct threads that tend to bind us all together despite the very diverse individuality of each member. Or perhaps because of it.

Some music historians would interject that it is incredible that we would ever know, or perhaps even like each other, let alone spend all of these years in such a productive atmosphere. Again, I credit the common threads.

More of them exist than what I have written about on these pages. The Oaks are as different from one another as night is from day.

Yet, the Great Creator has woven this tapestry together and decided in His infinite love and mercy to bless us beyond our dreams. That is why it is no small wonder that one of the most common threads that weaves together the Oak Ridge Boys is an incredible love and respect for Southern-style, Gospel quartet music.

Each "Oak" was heavily influenced at a very young age by many of the great Southern Gospel groups, such as the Blackwood Brothers, the Statesmen, the Cathedrals, the Couriers, the Speer Family, and yes, the Oak Ridge Quartet.

Hearing these groups sing made us all realize that we wanted to someday sing in, well . . . a quartet! Gospel music is what helped each of us chart a course for our future during that early part of our youth when most kids have no idea where their ship is heading.

I believe that in order to fully understand the Oak Ridge Boys, and what we are all about, you must let your mind's eye look back a bit into the past. It is always the past that helps us to define where we are now and where we might be going in the future.

Please allow me to guide you back into the Oak Ridge Boys' historical archives for just a few

Willie Wynn, Tommy Fairchild, William Golden, Smitty Gatlin and Herman Harper, early 1960s.

moments. It is a very interesting story that dates back to 1945, when a country bluegrass group from Knoxville, Tennessee, known as the Georgia Clodhoppers, began to visit the secret nuclear installation in Oak Ridge.

This was during the closing days of World War II. The war in Europe had ended but the Japanese were showing no sign of surrender and if something extraordinary wasn't done soon, many more thousands of young American lives would be lost in the Pacific.

The extraordinary answer to the world's problem was the "Manhattan Project," the building of two atomic bombs, which would eventually be dropped right on top of the cities of Hiroshima and Nagasaki, Japan, and bring a brutal end to an already brutal war.

One of the secret government sites was in the town of Oak Ridge, Tennessee, where thousands of workers toiled in secret. They were all sequestered for many months inside this installation. Scientists, physicists, engineers, military personnel, civilian specialists of all kinds, as well as their families. All hard at work, focused, and at times, bored beyond comprehension.

The Georgia Clodhoppers would become the only outside group ever allowed into the government installation at Oak Ridge. They would put on show after show for these brave Americans, usually on a Saturday. They would sing their country and bluegrass songs. But what the people really wanted – and needed to hear in this time of historical stress – were songs of the Gospel. And the Clodhoppers obliged.

Eventually they would become known to the folks there as Our Oak Ridge Quartet, and when the war ended, they changed their name to just that — the Oak Ridge Quartet.

In 1948, they started the Friday Night Singing Convention in Nashville on WSM Radio's Grand Ol' Opry. They became a very successful group, touring constantly throughout the South. They disbanded around 1955 and a year or so later, four young guys reorganized the group and hit the road again.

THE DEACON AND FRIENDS

At a recent show, an 82-year-old Lon "Deacon" Freeman joined us on stage to sing a few Gospel songs.

"The Deacon," who lived in Georgia, was a member of the original Oak Ridge Quartet out of Knoxville, Tennessee. So there I was, a 29-year member of a group singing on stage with an 82-year-old man who had sung in the same group all those years ago. Wow!

After the show, "the Deacon" said, "Well, one thing hasn't changed, the Oak Ridge Boys always did rock the house!"

Somewhat mind-boggling, it was one of the greatest nights I can remember as an Oak.

Perhaps, some day some younger guys will keep this tradition going, and maybe some day an eighty-two-year-old Joe Bonsall will join them on stage and "rock the house!"

Hey, it could happen!

Unfortunately, we lost the Deacon in the summer of 2003. We also lost our dear friend and former bass singer Noel Fox last summer. Smitty Gatlin, as well as Herman Harper, have also passed on. We will see all of these Boys again someday in glory!

Lon Freeman inducted with the Oak Ridge Boys into the Gospel Music Hall of Fame.

To avoid confusion with the quartet, this new group eventually started calling themselves the Oak Ridge Boys. Very few American music acts have this kind of long and enduring history.

William Lee Golden first joined the Oaks in 1965, replacing Jim Hamill, who had replaced Gary McSpadden in 1964, who had replaced Ron Page in 1962.

Duane Allen joined the group in 1966, after singing for a year with the Prophets Quartet out of Knoxville, Tennessee. He replaced Smitty Gatlin.

Richard Sterban started singing the bass for the Oaks in 1972, replacing Noel Fox, who had replaced Herman Harper.

I joined in 1973, replacing one of the most popular tenors to ever grace a Gospel music stage, Little Willie Wynn.

Although the four of us are the ones that America identifies as the Oak Ridge Boys, we owe much to those who have held the banner high, long before any of us became members. Each of us has the unique experience of having been huge fans of the Oaks long before we ever joined!

As a Gospel disc jockey in 1964, Duane Allen chartered a bus full of listeners from his hometown of Paris, Texas, and took them to a live concert performance of the Oaks in Fort Worth.

From the time a young Bill Golden from Brewton, Alabama, first heard the Oak Ridge Boys' Warner Brothers albums, *Folk-Minded Spirituals For Spiritual-Minded Folk* and *Sounds Of Nashville,* he saw himself as a member of the group. He followed that vision and never let it fade.

As young singers from the Philadelphia area, Richard and I pretty much believed that the Oak Ridge Boys were the most innovative and energetic group that we had ever seen, and we still cannot believe that we eventually became a vital part of its history!

The Oak Ridge Boys take our marvelous history to the stage each night and although our music has expanded quite a bit over the years, one cannot deny the influence of that Southern Gospel, four-part harmony in each song that we sing, no matter what the genre may be.

Just listen to some mighty big Oaks' standards, like "Dig a Little Deeper in the Well," "Everyday," "You're the One," "Touch a Hand," "It Takes a Little Rain," and "Thank God for Kids," just to name a few.

It is always Gospel music that reflects our roots and our beginnings and Gospel music is still the address where our heritage resides. To a man, I can honestly say it is still — and will always be — our first love.

The Oak Ridge Boys have been called "a Gospel quartet singing country music with a rock-and-roll attitude," and I would say that describes our music and style pretty well. I do know that there is no other entertainment act quite like us anywhere out there and that is an incredible blessing.

Another common and important thread, as stated before, is the fact that all four Boys possess

(above) The Oaks pose with their first Grammy. Members at the time were (top row) Duane Allen, Noel Fox, William Lee Golden; (bottom row) Tommy Fairchild (keyboard), and Willie Wynn.

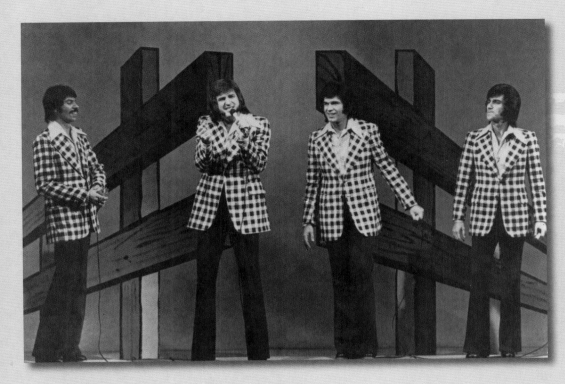

a deep respect and an endearing love for the very group itself. That is why I can write objectively about the Oaks. Even though I have been singing here for over thirty years, I am also a huge fan.

When people come up to us and exclaim, "I have loved you guys since I was a kid," I always take it as a huge compliment.

Sometimes I'll joke around and say something like, "Well, the Oaks have been singing since the day the earth began to cool." But down deep in the heart of each of us, we have never taken one moment of our success with this group for granted.

Each person who has taken the time out of their lives to come out and hear us sing our songs is precious to us. Consider this: the Boys are back in town, tickets are on sale. The local radio stations, newspapers, and TV stations all devote a little time to the coming appearance of the Oak Ridge Boys. More than likely folks have heard Richard or me talking to the local DJ from a phone in a hotel room several days before. They may have read an interview with Duane Allen or William Lee Golden in the Sunday supplement of the paper.

Say a family of four in Galveston, Texas, makes plans to go and see the show. Perhaps they invite Grandma to go as well. So, Mr. Smith buys five tickets to the show. The family plans to pick up Granny and go out to dinner and make a night of it.

Meanwhile, at the concert hall, the Oaks' crew is busy unloading the truck and setting up the sound and lights for tonight's performance. The Oaks and band are at the Holiday Inn. Each man woke up on the bus in his own time and made his way to his room to call home, check e-mail, have a bite to eat, and clean up for the show.

29

On many days, if the weather is nice, some of the Boys might decide to take a long walk around town. Not just for the exercise either. It is fun to get a feel of the town before the show. I may find myself on such a walk when a minivan drives by with the family and Grandma. The hard-working father rolls down his window and yells to me, "Welcome to town, we're all going to hear you tonight!"

That family will spend their hard-earned money on tickets, dinner, tips, and parking. They will more than likely buy a few tee shirts or bucket hats, and perhaps a copy of this book. After the show, they might stop by the merchandise table again and pick up a few CDs.

They will clap their hands, sing along, and in so doing, welcome the Oak Ridge Boys to their town! We, in turn, will attempt to give them every ounce of energy we have on that stage, because we are genuinely honored that they are out there.

That family is never taken for granted. The Oak Ridge Boys want that family and all of the rest of the audience to be glad they came and each man will do all in his power to make sure that the show does just that.

We will sing the hits. We will sing some Gospel. We will sing some patriotic-flavored songs, and even pick a little bluegrass. We will have a few laughs, and we will share a small piece of our lives with those who have cared enough to share some of themselves and their town with us.

We all feel this way in our hearts. It is one more common thread that binds us together. It may be the most important thread, because this shared philosophy may be the main reason why, year after year, decade after decade, the Oak Ridge Boys are still coming to your town. Perhaps, since you were a kid!

All of this is a vital part of our threads and beginnings, as well as whatever future there will be for the Oak Ridge Boys. This legacy *will* continue. I can almost guarantee it!

Television has always been an important aspect of the Oaks' career.

A Mother's Perspective

Despite the fact that Lillie Bonsall worked hard for her children and supported Joe both financially and emotionally in his quest for professional music, she said, "He's given us much more than we ever gave him. I've got the best son in the whole world." Lillie and her husband, Joe Sr., passed away a few years ago, and were featured in their son's bestselling book, *G.I. Joe and Lillie*. Their son and daughter, Nancy, were the joys of their lives. All remembered fondly "Joey's" road to stardom.

Lillie remembered that Joe was a "ham" [editor's note to fans: has anything changed?] as a child. "I would come home from work when he was two or three years old and Joey would be singing; his Nannie taught him a new song each day."

Joe Sr. took Joey to Gospel sings in the Pennsylvania area, and that propelled him to the career that would make him famous. "Joey would always say, 'Mom, someday you're going to be proud of me. I'll have my name in lights and ride a big bus.' "

Lillie's favorite song to hear Joe sing was also her favorite song that the Oak Ridge Boys recorded — "I Guess It Never Hurts to Hurt Sometime."

It's never too late to *learn!*

First of all I must admit to having always appreciated bluegrass music. My goodness, the Oak Ridge Boys once recorded a version of "Blue Moon Of Kentucky" with the "Father of Bluegrass," Bill Monroe.

However, I must also admit that I have never developed a real love for bluegrass until the last several years. On more than one occasion, I have referred to the "great bluegrass scare of '84." That is the year that bluegrass music came to the forefront for a while, just as it has done recently with the success of the *Oh, Brother* soundtrack album.

I guess I was afraid it might take over. It didn't. It might take over now, and I would be comfortable with that. The earth revolves. Attitudes and tastes morph and change — a good thing.

That ever swinging pendulum of country music continues to swing between a roots sound and more of a pop sound, as it has done for decades. And if the truth be known, it is this constant swing of creativity that keeps the music fresh and interesting.

As long as there is energy behind the music, I like it! Throughout my career as a Gospel singer and country hit maker with the Oaks, I have given my stage career every ounce of energy that I possess. And, to me, that is what the rock-and-roll attitude is all about.

So, I guess I am a rocker at heart, but that moniker doesn't always describe the music I like. Instead, as I said, to me rock and roll reflects an attitude. An energy level, if you will, that takes any genre of music to more of an exciting level — whether it's Gospel, country, or polka music.

Have you ever seen the Jimmy Sturr Polka Band? Their music may not be everyone's cup of tea, but I guarantee you, those guys are great! They rock and yes, the Boys have even recorded with Sturr. Won a Grammy, too. A polka Grammy!

My musical tastes have always varied. My CD player contains a wide range of stuff. I love the garage band, backbeat, sax-driven sounds of Springsteen and Seger, as well as the fresh country sounds of an Emmylou Harris or the Nitty Gritty Dirt Band. I love Andre Bocelli, as well as the Dixie Chicks. I listen to Josh Groban, as well as Merle

33

BAN-JOEY

OR:

HOW A PHILLY BOY CAME TO LOVE THE

FIVE-STRING BANJO

Haggard. As of late, I have been listening to a ton of bluegrass, which brings me back to the banjo.

The first banjo music that I ever heard was as a kid. That strange Philadelphia phenomenon called the string band, as in mummers. One hundred guys wearing feathers and strumming banjos is quite an assault and, although I got a kick out of the pomp and fun of these groups as a child, I never aspired to put on a pair of purple tights and a headdress and march down Market Street strumming my brains out.

I also grew up in the folk era, and I did love the Kingston Trio. I even had the 45 RPM singles of songs like "Tom Dooley" and "MTA." And I did enjoy the banjo energy possessed by the little bald guy. But, again, I never wanted to strap on a banjo and sing "Kumbaya" or "500 Miles Away from Home" as my life's work either.

Joe, dancin' the
night away.

I have gone for decades without ever once thinking about playing the banjo. To me, the banjo just floated around out there somewhere in musical space occupying some of the same air as a mandolin or perhaps a dulcimer. Appreciated for its occasional flavor, but not loved.

Last summer I occupied a first-class seat on a flight across the USA from Los Angeles to Nashville

with a real, live banjo player. First came the obligatory banjo jokes.

"You never see a banjo player in a Porsche," etc. etc.

Actually, Banjo Boy had the best one. "Hear the one about the banjo player who won the lottery? He just kept pickin' till the money ran out!" BA-Boom!

We had a real good time.

We started talking serious banjo on that flight. I admitted that I had always appreciated the energy of the banjo. The rolls and licks that come off a well-played five-string can really be exciting. I told him how I had always appreciated players like Bela Fleck, Buck Trent, and John McCuen, and I told him that one of my favorite albums of the last several years was the Steve Earle bluegrass album with the Del McCoury Band.

He told me that I should look into trying to play someday. He assured me that I would love it. Then he grabbed his banjo gig case from the compartment above and said goodbye and good luck. As he disappeared into Foggy Mountain Breakdown land, my creative wheels started to turn — always dangerous.

Could I play a banjo?
Could I pick?
Could I?
Maybe . . . could be fun.

The only pick and roll I had been accustomed to was in the game of basketball, and I must admit I was apprehensive about stepping on out there and actually buying an instrument. Then a few more events took place that pushed me on over the banjo-playing precipice.

The Oaks were backstage at the Grand Ol' Opry and the Ricky Skaggs band was off in a side room standing in a semi-circle working on a few tunes. I approached them, and Ricky invited me to stand right there amongst them and listen. They even started to play just for me. So there I was, smack in the middle of the greatest players in the universe, and I heard the banjo up close and felt the seamless relation of the instrument as it blended its sound into those of the guitars and mandolin and such. In that moment of space and time, I knew that I wanted to learn to play the banjo. Over I went.

I had actually bought a few bluegrass-flavored albums in the weeks proceeding that night at the Opry, so I guess I knew this was coming. I was listening to the new Chick's *Home* album and loving it, as well as some Allison Krauss and a new Del McCoury Band album, as well as a few others.

Truth be known, I was searching for Ricky that night, and I found what I was looking for.

"Hey now, this is fun stuff."

I really liked the energetic sound. It moved me on to the next level of banjo being.

In September of 2002, I popped the question.

"Mary?. . . Honey? Can I have a banjo for an anniversary present?"

It was a funny moment that resulted in my first ever banjo. A reasonably priced Gibson Epiphone that retailed for $900. I now play a custom-made Gibson and a brand new all-American banjo . . . the Deering Tenbrooks!

I love my banjo. I play every day and have for almost two years. I now live in a world of instructional CDs and videos, as well as some really good banjo books. I, of course, have the required Earl Scruggs Book. All banjo playing comes from the womb of Earl.

I have run into many guys who play and have helped me along the way. Most recently I have learned a few good licks from Jimmy Fortune, Matt Gilliam, and Billy Radar, as well as some real cool teachers like Danny Yancey, Dean Holman, Ross Nickerson, and Murphy Henry. I find myself surfing the 'net for banjo web

Joseph Sloan Bonsall

sites and forums and lessons and, yes, there are a lot of them out there. My favorites being www.banjohangout.com and www.banjoteacher.com

I spend many hours on my farm or in hotel rooms or in the back lounge of the bus practicing my banjo. Forward rolls, backward rolls, alternate thumb rolls, reverse rolls. Chords up and down the neck. Songs, techniques, lick after lick. It is not always pretty but I keep on pickin'.

Steve Martin once said that he practiced in his car with the door closed so that no one would be bothered by the sound of learning, which can be pretty hair raising. Just ask my cats. The first time I sat in my den and started to play, my wife said, "Oh, now I know why all the cats are in the upstairs closet, all wide eyed and shaking." That hasn't changed!

Ban-Joey is and always will be a work in progress, and I am diligently learning how to really play. I am actually playing a few songs from our new CD, *The Journey*, onstage with the band — and loving it.

No one in my family or any of my friends ever pictured me playing the old banjer — or writing books for that matter. Ban-Joey has been blessed!

Signing copies of the inspirational book *G.I. Joe and Lillie.*

GODFATHER

Jim Halsey has spent over 50 years in the entertainment business. In 1990, the Jim Halsey Company, Inc. was the number-one country music agency in the world, representing 41 top country and pop acts. Roy Clark, Waylon Jennings, the Judds, Merle Haggard, Reba McEntire, Clint Black, Freddy Fender, Roy Orbison, Tammy Wynette, Rick Nelson, Dwight Yoakam, Minnie Pearl, and many others have all benefited from Jim's expertise and positive thinking.

Chapter Four

I call it my Crossroads Theory, and I have actually written about it many times before.

The first time was when our longtime manager and "godfather," Jim Halsey, asked me to write the foreword for his critically acclaimed book, *How To Make It In The Music Business*.

Students of Dr. Halsey from all around the world have used this manual and memoir as a viable tool in helping them to understand the inner workings and behind-the-scenes mastery of the entertainment world, and I am honored to have a few of my words included in this must-read book.

I also alluded to my Crossroads Theory in my inspirational, biographical story, *G.I. Joe and Lillie*, published by New Leaf Press in 2003.

The theory? Simple!

I believe there are many times in your life that you consciously, or even unconsciously, arrive at a meaningful crossroad where an event takes place that tends to mold, shape, and influence the rest of your life on Earth.

Sometimes it is merely a simple decision that we make in our hearts or minds to take the right road instead of the left. Or, to choose the right thing to do instead of the wrong.

Many of these decisions we make are simple and very self-directed. Most, however, are Divine interventions, where God in His infinite wisdom has a definite plan for your life. But you must possess an open mind and an open heart to be aware of what it is that God is trying to tell you. So many missed opportunities exist because we just weren't listening.

I believe in my heart that at the most meaningful crossroads, God places a human being right there on the fork of the road at the appropriate time. A special human being whose influence changes our hearts and our very direction forever.

You will read the name "Jim Halsey" throughout this narrative. A story of the Oak Ridge Boys would be incomplete without him. In fact, without him, there would not be this story of the Oak Ridge Boys.

We call him "godfather." He has been the single most influential human being in the career and the lives of the Oaks. He is our spiritual leader, our advisor, our mentor, and most importantly, our dear friend.

We found ourselves at a huge crossroad in 1974 and 1975. The Oaks were starving to death and existing in a very gray area. We felt like we had the talent to really make a mark on the mainstream country music industry, but most radio deejays and concert promoters had a tendency to regard us as "just" a Gospel group and, therefore, refused to take us seriously.

These were the days when we rode the fence musically trying to appease everyone. We still sang a lot of Gospel songs (as we do today), but our attempt at branching out musically consisted of warm and fuzzy songs that were still somewhat Gospel in nature: about the sun and the stars and such.

Although some of these songs were really cool, we just couldn't seem to gain any real traction. (Our recording of "The Baptism of Jesse Taylor" *did* win a Grammy, though!)

The Oaks "before Joe" (circa 1972)

It was only our energetic, take-no-prisoners stage show that kept our heads above water. But our timepiece was quickly running out of sand.

We had been a cutting edge and innovative Gospel group, but the Southern Gospel music audiences in the mid-seventies were turning against us. We had played in Las Vegas with Johnny Cash; therefore, we had sinned greatly. And besides that, our hair was too darn long. And even worse, we didn't dress alike.

The future is always bright: the Oak Ridge
Boys made a move toward country music
in the early 1970s.

We took heat no matter what we did, so we stepped on out and away from the world that we knew, right into the abyss of a world that we didn't know. It was not an easy transformation. We really needed help.

Jim Halsey was standing at the crossroad. His Halsey Company management and booking agency out of Tulsa, Oklahoma, had already become the stuff of legend. Jim was the guiding hand behind the huge careers of Roy Clark, Mel Tillis, Minnie Pearl, and Tammy Wynette as well as legends like Hank Thompson — and as an old *Billboard* reads, "many others."

In the 70s and 80s, Jim's booking agency was an influential and far-reaching force that controlled the vast majority of dates played by all of the major artists of that era. From the showrooms of Las Vegas, to fairs, corporate events, package tours of all kinds, and huge music festivals all over the world, Jim's incredible group of seasoned agents could get you there. To be a part of the Halsey stable of talent garnered an incredible amount of respect as well as a great shot at success.

Jim's management service included career guidance, decision-making, counseling, and more!

The Halsey agency contacted our office in the spring of 1975 with a request. They needed an opening act on two dates because someone had canceled. A Friday night date in Warwick, Rhode Island, opening for Mel Tillis. And the next night, a Saturday night gig in North Tonawanda, New York, opening for Roy Clark. Tommy Overstreet would also be on these shows, so they would need about 20 minutes on each show from the Oak Ridge Boys.

Always innovative, from a high-energy, high-production show to international touring.

41

William Lee Golden, Joe Bonsall, record producer Ron Chancey, Duane Allen, Richard Sterban

Well, our date book was pretty wide open and, although it appeared that there wasn't a whole lot of money involved, we saw this as a tremendous opportunity. We jumped at the chance.

We all traveled in one bus back in those days. We called it *Chocolate* because it was a gold-and-brown-colored Silver Eagle. And we happily boarded the bus that Thursday afternoon to make a beeline toward New England.

We had recently performed at a wonderful event called the *American Song Festival* in Saratoga Springs, New York, where we performed a song called "Plant A Seed" for a compilation recording. The show was also seen on syndicated television and was really a fun gig. We had purchased new suits for that event, and we had them with us for Warwick, Rhode Island.

We hit the stage before Tommy Overstreet and Mel Tillis, all dressed out in these two-piece, modern gray suits — complete with open-collared shirts, orange-colored neck scarves (yes, I said *neck scarves*), and matching black platform shoes with two-inch heels on them.

Well, it was a revolving stage in the round, which presented a small challenge for the shoes, but we got through the show without being slung off into the audience. Actually, we did good. We knocked it down. We gave them 20 minutes of four-part Gospel harmony, the likes of which had never been seen on a country music stage.

I am happy to say that Tommy Overstreet, Mel Tillis, and the members of their bands made us feel welcome as well. It was a great night. We boarded the bus and partied all the way to the Niagara frontier of western New York.

It came to pass that word reached Jim Halsey about the success of our performance, and he immediately made plans to head for Tonawanda to see for himself. Well, we burned it up again. The Melody Fair stage was also a revolving round stage, and we now had a little more experience wearing platform shoes while singing and moving in a circle!

We spun around in front of Jim Halsey and sang our tails off while looking, well . . . tall!

In the words of Bob Seger, "We were young and strong and running against the wind!"

We were also broke.

"Ace" producers
Duane Allen and Ron
Chancey fine—tune the
Oaks' singular sound.

We met with Jim after the show and that is where he gave us his famous "Three-Minute Speech" that has become a part of music folklore.

"You have the best show that I have ever seen. I believe that you guys are just three minutes away from being superstars." The three minutes referring to a hit record.

He told us a lot more in that first meeting backstage. Our little talk with Jim Halsey that night meant more to the future of the Oak Ridge Boys than any other single moment in our history.

Here are a just a few pearls . . .

"We have to get you some work immediately, to help you pay some bills and give you confidence."

"You have to start singing some real country songs. Get off the fence and go for it."

Rockin' the house!

"I'll go to work on that record deal immediately."

"The Oaks will be a household name someday."

Then, a wonderful moment that would define our relationship over the coming decades. He bowed his head and stretched out both arms towards us. He grabbed a few hands and said, "Everyone stand here quietly in this circle and hold hands with each other for just a moment. Feel each other's energy. We need to pull together as one spirit and one force and ask for God's blessings to make this work."

Jim Halsey, our godfather, the man who would guide our career from this day forward, led us in a word of prayer.

In all these passing years, this has never changed!

One of our favorite venues: backstage at "The Tonight Show," with Jim Halsey, Judi Pofsky and Dick Howard of the Jim Halsey Company.

Got a minute?

In the early 90s the Oak Ridge Boys found ourselves floundering just a bit with RCA records. We had experienced some success there with a few hit songs like "Lucky Moon," and we had even recorded some pretty cool albums, which contained some cutting-edge and relevant music. However, we struggled.

In part, because there was a regime change going on at the top, and we just didn't seem to be included in their plans. We persevered there for a while — because, as always, we believed in our music. It was, however, hard to believe in RCA.

They wouldn't let us record "Achy Breaky Heart" ("too silly"), "She Is His Only Need" ("not for you"), or "I'm in a Hurry" ("too frantic"). All three songs became career moments for the likes of Billy Ray Cyrus, Wynonna Judd, and Alabama, respectively.

Jim Halsey was officially retired at this time and in fact wore the emeritus title, which when roughly translated from the ancient Roman means "retired." *But* . . .

At our request, Jim showed up at a huge pow-wow with the RCA brass, and he came armed with a heck of an idea. However, for a while, he just sat and said nothing. Small talk and a few jokes took place. I suggested an album idea: We take a

picture in gangster suits and hold a gun to the RCA dog, Nipper's head and title it, "Buy This or We'll Shoot the Dog!"

They actually thought I was serious! As they were talking about animal rights activists being upset, I interrupted and added, "Well, we could put a photo of the head of the label in the middle of the shot and say, "Buy it or we'll shoot him!"

They were not amused. This meeting was going downhill fast when all of a sudden Jim Halsey yells, "GOT A MINUTE?" and jumps up on top of the table.

I kid you not. He rose up and did a little boo-gie dance with all the RCA brass looking up at him. They thought it was outrageous. It was!!!

He jumped down, landing right in front of the label head and proceeded to tell everyone that the Oaks should record just one minute of a song and release it that way.

Research showed that a one-minute record would be the shortest in history. The gimmick idea alone would garner tons of press and if a big country station will not play it . . . we buy one-minute spots all over the place and force them to play it. The spots would start out with the catch phrase, "Got a minute? . . . for the Oak Ridge Boys." A chain reaction would start. and the fallout would be huge! *Huge!*

RCA huffed and puffed and guffawed and said, "We'll get back to you."

They filed out of the boardroom shaking their heads.

I am not putting down RCA here. It is a legendary institution that has proven itself to be one of the greatest labels in history. After all, RCA had Elvis, for crying out loud.

I am just saying that this particular group of leaders, at that particular time, had no vision for the Oaks. When we left RCA later that year, it was an excellent move. Jim Halsey was with us as we went out the door. He kicked his shoes against the wall in a biblical fashion, in order to "remove the dust of this place" from his feet. We all rolled on the floor laughing.

Old proverb . . . "it is better to not be on a record label than to be with one that is NOT behind you." Going with RCA had proven to be a big mistake. One of the few that we have ever made.

Fast forward to the late 90s. Our old producer Ron Chancey and the Boys are in the studio again recording some great new music on an album called Voices, which we recorded for the Platinum record label. Jim didn't dance on the table this time, but he made an incredible presentation by bringing back his "Got a minute" idea. (I was shocked that somebody over at RCA hadn't used it by now... "Got a minute for Alabama's 'I'm in a Hurry?' " Phewww!)

Our longtime friend Kix Brooks of Brooks and Dunn had written a song for us many years ago that Duane Allen dug up out of his magical archives. The Ace never loses or forgets a good song. If we liked it once, we might like it again. He must have in his possession a huge bag of these songs that he keeps tucked inside of a very special place at his house. The man absolutely *never* forgets a well-written piece of material.

The song, "Baby When Your Heart Breaks Down" was a catchy little tune that featured every element of the standard Oaks' song. Ace on lead and with a sing along up-tempo chorus that just kept on coming at you. A very commercial record.

The "Got a minute for the Oak Ridge Boys?" promotion went into full gear as we released a brightly mixed sixty-second version of the song to the press and to radio.

All of a sudden the Oaks found ourselves bombarded with press. We were on television a bunch. Every show from "The Tonight Show" to the daytime "Donnie and Marie Osmond Show" wanted to talk to the Oak Ridge Boys about the "shortest record in history." It was even written up in USA Today. The song garnered tons of airplay as well. We eventually released the full version to radio.

You see, Jim Halsey never forgets a good idea either. So, heed some advice. If the Godfather ever calls you for a meeting . . . you had better "give him a minute."

Just keep him away from the furniture!

"THE GODFATHER," JIM HALSEY

IN PROPOSING THE OAKS' TRANSITION TO A CROSSOVER SOUND, JIM HALSEY MADE THE BOYS AN OFFER THEY COULDN'T REFUSE!

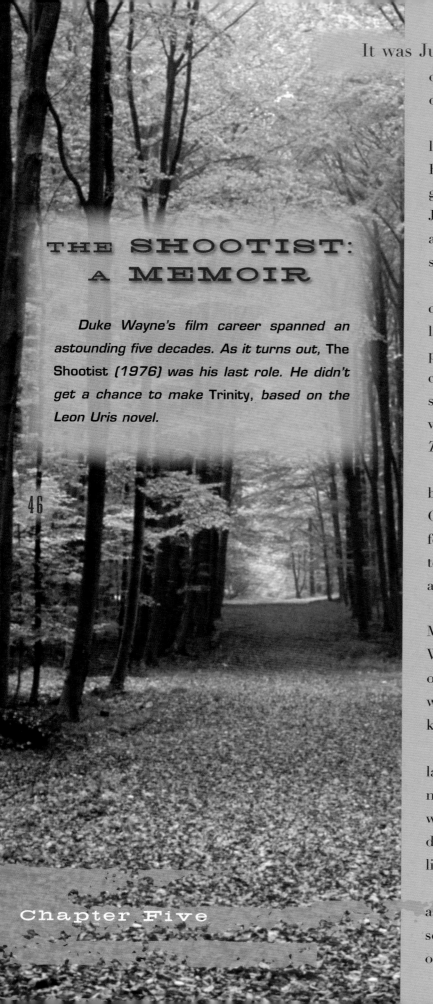

THE SHOOTIST: A MEMOIR

Duke Wayne's film career spanned an astounding five decades. As it turns out, **The Shootist** *(1976) was his last role. He didn't get a chance to make* Trinity, *based on the Leon Uris novel.*

46

Chapter Five

It was July of 2001 and the Oaks were in the middle of the same "Never Ending Tour" that has lasted for decades.

I was in a motel room in Mattoon, Illinois, where later on that evening we would play at the Bagel Festival before 14,000 folks from the heartland. I was glancing through a morning paper and noticed that John Wayne's last movie, *The Shootist*, was now available on DVD. How cool! Widescreen with digital sound.

It is amazing how such a seemingly small event can trigger a virtual flood of memories. I fired up the laptop, logged on to good old America Online and proceeded directly to Amazon.com and ordered a copy of this wonderful old western for each of my singing partners, as well as myself. They were each very happy to receive their very own DVD copy of *The Shootist*. Here is the reason why.

It was the summer of 1976, and the Oaks were booked for a solid week at a fair in Red Deer, Alberta, Canada. Our job was to sing on the grandstand stage for 30 minutes each night before the featured event took place. One night it was a rodeo, another night a circus, tractor pull, or demolition derby.

We were the music act as well as the Grand Marshals of a parade celebrating this annual event. We rode down the main street waving from the top of a stagecoach. Most folks had no idea who we were, but it didn't seem to matter. We felt like the kings of Alberta and played it to the hilt.

Incidentally, Red Deer is the home of Canada's largest institution for the mentally challenged. Each night they brought in several hundred of these folks with varying degrees of incapacity and sat them down right in front of us. I am in no way making light here — quite to the contrary.

To this very day, I remember this experience as being among the saddest sights that I have ever seen from a stage. All kinds of folks with all kinds of problems. People who could not keep still to the

Ron Howard and John Wayne in *The Shootist*

point that they wore football helmets to keep from hurting themselves or someone else. Or even worse, some unfortunate folks who were laid out in what looked like huge road cases, looking up at us and not moving a muscle.

I would be less than honest if I didn't tell you that some of this was kind of strange, however, the Boys performed as well as we could each evening and gave each 3o-minute show all the energy that we could muster, considering that we were a long way from home, with no money, and opening up for a guy who rode a motorcycle inside of a cage while eating hot dogs and playing a trumpet.

But overall, we tried to make the very best of this week in Red Deer, Alberta.

There was a softball field across from the hotel and each day we would practice. For years

we carried around bags of softball equipment. Gloves, bats, bases, balls. Some acts played golf, but we played softball. We had a decent little team and played a lot of games against radio stations or local police and firemen for charity. We won most of them, too. Our team was called the ORBITS, which stood for *Oak Ridge Boys Is Tough Stuff*!

So, each day guys that felt like playing would arrive at this pretty little park to spend a good part of the day tossing the ball around and shagging flies. But it was *The Shootist* that occupied our evenings.

The first VCR had just been invented and our young production manager and chief bottle washer, Jon Mir, owned one. To this very day, it is Jon Mir who constantly leads us down the pathway of technology and this early effort was well received and very exciting. Jon had the first Sony Betamax machine, perhaps, on the planet. And it was just about the coolest thing that we had ever seen. The possibilities of this new technology were mind-boggling.

Each night after the show, we would take this huge Betamax machine out of the bus and carry it into the hotel. It took at least two guys to carry it and a staff from MIT to figure out how to hook the thing up to the television.

The hotel was kind enough to provide a meeting room for us for the entire week. We did a little rehearsing there on some days, but at night we turned it into our own private movie theater. We would even arrange the seats in a big semi-circle in front of the TV. Every single one of us would attend this event and it was really fun.

The only problem was, we only had *one* movie — *The Shootist*.

It was the only one we needed.

I don't know how Jon obtained it because, remember, this was long before Blockbuster, and a movie on tape was unheard of. Only the very rich had big screens and projectors in their homes and watched movies on film. The VCR would eventually change everything.

The Shootist had been in the theaters just a month earlier so we felt like the cats that had just eaten the canary. This gritty western was the last one that John Wayne would ever make, and it also featured Jimmy Stewart, Richard Boone, Hugh O'Brian, a big Opie, (Ron Howard) and Lauren Bacall. It was a classic.

The Oak Ridge Boys watched that movie at least ten times in that Red Deer week alone, and we became experts on *The Shootist*. We talked about little else. Everyone had his own, bad John Wayne imitation that we all thought was pretty darn good.

I honestly believe that every man in America at one time or another believes he can do John Wayne, Jimmy Stewart, Elvis, or even Sylvester Stallone on any given day. ("Yo, Adrian!")

In Red Deer, each of us had the entire screenplay all but memorized. We knew every line uttered by "the Duke" in *The Shootist* and used them all in our daily conversations!

Well, you seem to have some real starch in your corset!

Well, you better find yourself another line of work!

It never stopped, even on stage between songs.

Why don't you just say it!

Well now, pardon me . . . Pilgrim!

For me there was even a deeper meaning. Little Joey Bonsall loved John Wayne, riding and shooting and saving the damsel, in those darkened Philly theaters. I once saw the movie, *The Commancheros*, nine times in one week at the old Midway Theater on Allegheny Avenue in Philadelphia.

I would take my Red Ryder pull wagon to the Acme supermarket on Kensington Avenue every morning and carry groceries home for little old ladies for a quarter a pop. I would actually take the bags into the house and help them put the stuff away.

When I earned enough money, *boom*, I took the wagon home and went to the movies. This scene would play out on many a summer day, especially on Saturdays. We had two neighborhood theaters, The Midway and The Iris, and I was a frequent customer at both of them. Sometimes I would have a few friends with me, but more times than not, I went all by myself.

Sometimes, when the Oaks have a night off on the road, I will go to a movie alone. It is a definite flashback to a little Joey sitting near the front of the theater (always near the front), gazing up the screen in a wide-eyed trance as the whole world would manifest itself right there in the Kensington section of Philadelphia.

The only difference now, except for the special effects that is, is that I am probably eating red Twizzlers and Goobers instead of Juicy Fruits and Black Crows. I never was a popcorn man, but I digress. . . .

Back to John Wayne. It was February of 1977, and the Oak Ridge Boys were heading for the Grammy Awards in Los Angeles. Not only was our song, "Where the Soul Never Dies," up for a Gospel Grammy, we were to host the presentations of the Gospel Grammies on network TV.

We were in San Antonio, Texas, the night before singing at a college buyers' showcase, hoping that we would put on a good enough show to be booked at Penn State or UCLA. We did well enough to secure a bunch of small college dates for the next year or so, and we never would play Penn State or UCLA. We had heard a rumor that John Wayne was speaking somewhere at the same event, but we never saw him.

We rose early and headed for the airport where, thanks to the Grammy Awards, we were to fly first class on American Airlines to Los Angeles. I believe this was the first time our group had ever flown first class. We had even been to the Soviet Union with Roy Clark a year before, but on that trip we were stuffed back in coach like sardines.

I boarded the plane and hung up my suit bag, containing my new white Harvey Krantz-designed outfit, in the front closet. I then proceeded to my seat in 1B.

We all had these fancy new customized suits for the award show. Our manager, Jim Halsey, wanted us to really stick out and we did. The suits all looked the same, except for a bunch of different colored squiggly western designs embroidered on the front and down the legs. Add a huge color-coordinated bow tie and frilly shirt and there you have it. We would look hideous on the Grammy Show!

Duane was across the aisle in 1C, Golden and Richard were right behind me, and 1A by the window was open.

Duane leaned over to me and whispered the following words. "Don't freak out man, keep your cool, but John Wayne is getting on this airplane."

WILLIAM LEE'S BEST COWBOY POSE.

Before I could ascertain whether or not the Ace was kidding around, I found myself popping up to allow the Duke into seat 1A. It *was* John Wayne, and I was freaking right on out!

He looked ten feet tall as he settled down into his seat and buckled his safety belt. I didn't say anything for a long time, and then, "Hello, sir."

John Wayne was bigger then life. I flashed back to my childhood as I tried not to stare at this real-life movie star in seat 1A.

Over the course of my career with the Oak Ridge Boys, I would meet many famous people — presidents, kings, the greatest sports stars who have ever lived, well-known television and movie stars, and music legends from every genre. However, I do not recall ever feeling quite as inspired by it all as I did on that airplane sitting next to the Duke.

So, after a while I got up a healthy dose of courage and introduced myself and the others to John Wayne.

He was wonderful to us. A man of his stature had to know what it meant

for us to meet him and get to chat a little, and he was so very gracious.

I can't tell you how emotional it was for me to sit next to this man, Remember now, the summer of *The Shootist* in Red Deer was only a few months before, but more than that, he was my hero.

I met Elvis once a few years before and that was a thrill, but I never actually chatted with Elvis. I remember every word John Wayne said in the front of that plane.

The flight attendant came by with some fruit and asked, "Mr. Wayne, would you like something?"

"I think I'd like to have an apple."

To this day, on any given moment, you will hear an Oak say, "I'd like to have an apple," in his best John Wayne voice.

His hands looked very old and it moved me to tears. I actually went to the bathroom and cried about it.

We talked about *The Shootist*. He was very happy with that movie. He identified well with the old gunfighter, John Books, who tried to retire to a small town and fight cancer.

I asked about his next film.

"Are you familiar with the novel *Trinity*?" he asked.

"I know the book sir, although I haven't read it," I answered, sounding as matter of fact as I could, considering that my insides continued to freak out.

"Well, I am going to play a mean, crusty, old son of a buck and that's not a hard part for me to play."

He laughed out loud, and we all laughed right along with him. At this point we had him pretty much surrounded, but eventually we all backed off and let John Wayne alone. He took a nap for most of the rest of the trip. He laid his head back and slept without making a sound. He didn't even drool. Richard sleeps like that.

When he awoke we were on approach to LAX, and I asked him for an autograph. I felt like a bonehead, but I just had to have something to memorialize this precious moment in time.

He signed a piece of paper for me. It read, "To Joe, Friendship, Duke Wayne."

I am not sure whatever happened to it. I think I may still have it hidden away in a box somewhere. Every time I sign a slip of paper for someone, I wonder what will happen to it.

John Wayne never made the movie, *Trinity*. He died of cancer in 1979.

So, today, I ordered four copies of *The Shootist* on DVD for me and my singing partners.

Addendum: The Oaks are tearing across the plains states in August of 2001 with the DVD of *The Shootist* playing in front of the bus at a massive volume. Everyone is talking like John Wayne again just like in 1976.

The world turns, the bus keeps going, the Boys keep singing.

The Oaks in the White House, 1979, with Jimmy and Rosalynn Carter.

Some things are somewhat different now. We have a much bigger bus and, of course, newer technology. Not only do we have laptops and DVD players, but we even have DVD players in our laptops.

We also have a Direct TV satellite system with hundreds of channels that actually works as we go down the road. This is the greatest thing to happen to road warriors since they first began to deliver pizzas to Holiday Inns in the early 80s.

Many things do NOT change. Our approach to singing and giving our show the best we have is no different from Red Deer in 1976. However, there are some events that seem to move about space and time in huge circles and keep coming back around over and over again. And *The Shootist* is just one small example.

I think I'd like to have an apple!

51

STONES ON THE MOUNTAIN

"Oaks, please, do not try to move! DO NOT even try to dance! Just stand still! Susan will move! You will NOT!"

Famous choreographer, Walter Painter, screaming when the Boys tried a dance scene with Susan Anton, while singing the Peaches and Herb song "Reunited" for a short-lived NBC network show called "The Mel [Tillis] and Susan Show." We looked like a wad of worms.

Chapter Six

It was a sunny and pivotal day in the career of the Oak Ridge Boys when we landed in Los Angeles, California. We had just met John Wayne on the airplane and we were already stoked!

Dick Howard met us at the LAX International Airport on this morning in February of 1977. He had pulled a miracle by booking the Oaks on a huge primetime slot on CBS Television as presenters and performers on the Grammy Awards show.

Many good things were about to happen as a result of this trip.

Dick Howard was the crackerjack television agent of the Jim Halsey Company and the man responsible for getting the Oak Ridge Boys all over the tube in the middle seventies and beyond.

What was truly remarkable was his ability to obtain important TV appearances for the Oaks in the days when we didn't have one single record on the charts. "Y'all Come Back Saloon" would hit later on in the fall of 1977, however, over the course of 1975 through 1977 and beyond, Dick Howard and Jim Halsey would make us the darlings of daytime TV — with 28 performances on "The Mike Douglas Show" alone. Sometimes, we would co-host this show with Mike Douglas a week at a time on location in places like Miami (and even London, England!).

We also performed regularly on the Dinah Shore and Merv Griffin shows. And we did our first "Tonight Show" with Johnny Carson during this period. We would go on to appear on that show over 30 times in the years to come.

"The Tonight Show" was always the one show that made our palms sweat. It always felt like the biggest of the big time to us, because *it was*! Right before Johnny would introduce us, we would stand behind that curtain and shake. I think it made us excel to a higher level, because there was no way we wanted to screw up on that show, especially with Johnny Carson sitting there at his desk looking at us.

53

The Oaks with Paul Simon

People have always wondered why we never sat down by the desk and talked with Johnny. We had read that he hated talking to music groups and, besides, we had seen some of our peers come off looking rather badly from time to time. So we would always just perform our two songs, shake Mr. Carson's hand and leave. (We heard once that Johnny had a lot of respect for us and that is why he always said yes when Dick Howard called.)

Television would be a huge part of our career thanks to Dick Howard. It never stopped. He was able to book us on shows like "The Dukes of Hazard," as well as many other award shows and network variety shows over the years (such as the Minnie Pearl Christmas specials on CBS and others).

We eventually performed on many popular music shows such as "Dick Clark's Rockin' New Years Eve, " "The Midnight Special," "Don Kirschner's Rock Concert," "Austin City Limits," "PBS Soundstage," as well as a dozen episodes of "Solid Gold." We also taped "Hee Haw" twice a year and performed regularly on all the Nashville shows such as "Pop Goes the Country," "Ralph Emery," "Crook and Chase," and "Prime Time Country."

Yes indeed, the Oaks did a lot of television, and it all really helped to solidify us as a nationally known act, especially once the hits started rolling out.

It is amazing that some 23 years after that Grammy appearance, Sherman Halsey would enlist the help of Dick Howard in the creation of our own weekly television show for The Nashville Network. Sherman is the son of our godfather, Jim Halsey, and he was the main force behind the 15 one-hour variety shows that played during prime time on Saturday nights. It was called "The Oak Ridge Boys Live from Las Vegas."

This was the most ambitious undertaking of our career. We taped 15 shows in less than two weeks at the Las Vegas Hilton. We had well over 60 guests, including everyone from Tim McGraw to a talking dog and Kenny Rogers to Charo.

It was hard work but well worth it. Sherman's big time production and direction made each show look like a separate concert event. The 15 shows and their many repeats garnered huge cable ratings, as well, and put the Oak Ridge Boys right back into people's living rooms again. The show reminded them, in a big time way, what we were all about.

Sherman Halsey worked hard and sacrificed much for this incredible project, and Dick was always nearby to lend a hand. I should add here that Sherman Halsey has directed three television specials for us over the

With the Captain and Tennille, and friend!

Television has played a major role in the Oaks' career.

last few years in cooperation with Reverend Larry Jones and Feed the Children. Under the godfather's leadership, we taped the "Inconvenient Christmas" special in 2002, the "Let Freedom Sing" patriotic special in 2003, and most recently a "Songs from the Heart" Gospel music special in early 2004.

There are plans for another special based on our new album, *The Journey*, slated for early 2005. What a great opportunity! Folks get to see us on stations like ABC Family, WGN, BET, PAX, and CBS, and we get to raise a lot of money for hungry children as well.

But back in those early days, it was Dick Howard who taught us how to use the medium of television to our advantage, and I would dread to think what our career might have been like without him. Dick passed away in the winter of 2001, and I assure you that if there is a *Heavenly Television Network* (HTN) the little Jewish boy from Manhattan is acting as someone's agent right now — and getting them a prime spot on a big show, even if nobody knows who they are!

We loved Dick. It was so much fun to mess with him. He called a big meeting once while we were in LA, and we all sat in front of his desk like four little boys listening to his thoughts and plans and ideas. He could go on and on forever.

Duane Allen says, "Hey Dick, I have to go to the bathroom."

We all decide at that very moment that a break for nature is in order, so we rise up as one and head down the hall for the men's room, leaving Dick sitting there in mid-sentence. After leaving the bathroom, we proceeded to the fire escape and down to the parking lot, where we got into our limo and drove off! We found out later that he sat there waiting for us for over an hour before he realized he was had. Jim Halsey

A serious "Hee Haw" moment.

On "The Mike Douglas Show."

told the story at his memorial service. We all miss Dick Howard.

But back to that day in the City of Angels in February 1977. Up to this point, we had not been on television very much and before the night was over we would appear on the most prestigious music show of the year — the "Grammy Awards."

Not only did we get a fabulous shot on network TV, but we won a Grammy for "Where the Soul Never Dies." But what was really cool was the fact that we became friends with Paul Simon.

Paul loved harmony groups. He had once used the Dixie Hummingbirds for backup vocals on his big hit, "Loves Me like a Rock."

We were mired down on Columbia records at the time, trying to decide a clear musical direction, so we found ourselves counseling with Simon that afternoon during rehearsals. The only revelation that came out of our talks ended up to be a huge one. We asked Paul Simon to write us a song, to which he replied, "I can't do that, Boys. I am a selfish man with my music and when I write a song, I have to be the one to sing it. But I'll call you if I think of something." He called the next week.

Paul Simon flew us up to New York (first class, too) and put us up at the Americana Hotel. We even had our own rooms and a food budget. Paul was producing a new rock act called the Roche Sisters, and he wanted us to sing background vocals on a few tracks. The songs weren't great but hey, man, we were inside the famous A&R Studios with Phil Ramone producing and Paul Simon directing. Nothing ever came of it except a memorable experience for all of us. I mean Billy Joel had cut *The Stranger* album in this place, and Paul Simon did all of his legendary recording here, as well. The soundtrack for *A Star Is Born* was recorded at A&R with Phil Ramone producing, so the Boys were indeed stepping around in some pretty high cotton.

We no sooner got back to Hendersonville, Tennessee, and Paul called us again.

"I want you to come back to New York as soon as you can. I just wrote a song and I want you to be on the record with me."

This time we sat around a circle in the famous A&R Studios with Paul Simon and sang "Slip Slidin' Away," which became a monster hit record by the end of that year. It was the only new song on a *Paul Simon Greatest Hits* compilation and there we were singing all the backup vocals.

57

A lot of folks didn't know that it was the Oak Ridge Boys singing on that record, but we knew it, and I will be eternally grateful to Paul Simon for not only the lessons learned and from sharing a bit of his genius, but for the incredible shot in the arm it gave our pride each time we heard "Slip Slidin' Away."

When we received a copy of Paul's gold album in appreciation, we hung it right up on the office wall. To this day, we refer to it as our first gold album, although we didn't have a thing to do with "Julio Down by the Schoolyard."

We heard that when Jim Halsey finally got us released from Columbia Records, one board member at the label, a Mr. Simon, stood up at a meeting and chastised the board for not doing more to hold on to the Oak Ridge Boys!

So, meeting Paul Simon was definitely the highlight of the Grammy awards that year. In the years to come, we would be on the Grammy show many times again. We would perform, present, and even take another one home – for "Elvira" in the *Country Record of the Year* category in 1981. And over the years, we would garner a dozen more nominations. But that first show was really something.

We also pulled off a huge public relations coup in the weeks that followed. When our four Grammy awards arrived in Hendersonville, they were all broken. Our publicist was Kathy Gangwisch, who had begun to work for us, via Jim Halsey, the year before. Kathy would be our publicist for 25 years and, like Jim Halsey and Dick Howard, would become a vital cog in the wheel throughout our career.

Together we came up with an idea. We took a casual photo of the Oaks holding their broken Grammys with a somewhat smirky, puzzled look on our faces. Kathy G. released the picture to the wire services with

this caption, "The Oak Ridge Boys, a Grammy apiece? OR a piece of a Grammy?" It was published in every newspaper and magazine in the country.

I have often thought that the mid-70s were the most pivotal years in the history of the Oak Ridge Boys. Yes, we were starving to death; however, we seemed to be constantly doing all the right things. Under Jim Halsey's leadership, we placed a lot of little stones on the pile that eventually became huge mountains.

Consider the trip to the Soviet Union with Roy Clark in January of 1976. Up until that trip, only Tennessee Ernie Ford had toured Soviet Russia as an American ambassador of goodwill through music. Thanks to Jim Halsey, Roy Clark and the Oaks would be the second American tour – many years before Billy Joel and Bon Jovi, as well as others, would perform there.

It was to be a three-week tour, worked out through both governments as part of a cultural exchange program, although we never figured out what the USA received in exchange for the Boys and Roy!

Jim worked out every detail. Before we left for Russia, we performed for ten days with Roy at the Frontier Hotel in Las Vegas, and a parade of Soviet diplomats came to every show. You see, it was *Communist* Russia in 1976. The Iron Curtain was still securely in place and the totalitarian government that Ronald Reagan eventually scared out of existence still controlled everything that was said or sung about in their country.

We had to submit lyrics for each song for approval by the KGB before they would allow us to go on in front of anyone. The only song that raised their eyebrows was our old Gospel song, "Where the Soul Never Dies." This song had won us a Gospel Grammy and we really wanted to sing it overseas.

The Soviets told us we could sing it if we would change the words from "to *Canaan Land* I'm on my way," to "to *Disneyland* I'm on my way"! — incredible but true! We compromised and sang, "To *that fair* land I'm on my way."

I guess the thought of Canaan Land set the Commies back a bit. We sure didn't want to start a war over it!

The trip was an incredible success. We performed a week in Riga Latvia, a week in the city that was then known as Leningrad, and a week in Moscow.

The Soviet people, although a bit dark and drab from the constant oppression, welcomed us with an incredibly warm response each and every night. Our four-part harmony went over big time. And Roy, along with banjo virtuoso Buck Trent, did things with musical instruments that they had never heard before.

It was a memorable event for each and every one of us, and it made us all better Americans. The difference between living in the "land of the free" and the land of "no freedom" was very stark and we all felt blessed for the experience.

Besides that, Jim Halsey and Kathy Gangwisch made sure that the press coverage was huge. If one read the newspapers, you would have thought Roy and the Oaks were responsible for changing the face of a whole Communist nation.

We may not have accomplished that, but we did, once again, prove that music is *indeed* a universal language. And the tour changed our lives forever.

What a way to begin 1976, a year that the USA would celebrate two hundred years as "one nation under God." Soviet Russia had been around for thousands of years and only in 1976 did they hear a Gospel quartet, as well as a banjo and a fiddle. (Before that, they actually believed one of those things was called a violin.) Hey, it might have been the beginning of the end for the Iron Curtain. Jim Halsey may be the greatest diplomat of all.

London: (left) Here we are at 10 Downing Street. Cool! (right) The Oaks' tenor prepares to take a dip in the Thames!

Oaks over the years with John R. Cash.

A word about Roy Clark. Our friendship with Roy, coupled with his willingness to take us along with him for a while, made a huge impact on the Oaks' career, as well as our personal lives. We toured over a good portion of America and the world with Roy.

Roy is a jovial and funny fellow who is in possession of a

heart of solid gold. He is also one of the finest musicians to ever grace a stage.

Roy was and is a pure professional in every sense of the word, and he helped us form some tremendous building blocks during some very gray and bleak times. We are grateful to Roy Clark, and we love him dearly.

From 1973 into 1976, the Oaks floundered around on Columbia records. We worked with some top producers like George Richey and Billy Sherrill and made some very good records. But our direction was still somewhat confusing, and from the standpoint of Columbia records, they just didn't know what to do with us.

Jim Halsey got us out of that contract and encouraged his longtime friend, the president of ABC-DOT records, Jim Foglesong, to take a chance on us. Halsey and Foglesong hooked us up with a hot young producer named Ron Chancey, and together we would end up making music history.

Ron came out to meet us that spring in Oklahoma City, at a venue called the Lincoln Plaza Dinner Theater. This was another venue that Jim used as a showcase for the Oaks, much like the Landmark Hotel in Vegas.

He would book us there for a week of shows and fly important buyers and promoters to the venue to see us. Jim and Dick Howard even managed to produce a syndicated Oak Ridge Boys' TV special from the Lincoln Park Theater. Again, way before the hits came.

Anyhow, we hit it off with Ron Chancey right away, and he headed straight back to Nashville to dig up some good songs. The first two he earmarked for the Oaks were a song from an old Glen Campbell album, called "You're the One in a Million," and a new song written by a lady named Sharon Vaughn, "Y'all Come Back Saloon."

1976 and 1977! What incredible years for the Oak Ridge Boys. The Soviet Union trip with Roy Clark, "Slip Slidin' Away," a new deal with ABC-DOT, (which was to morph into MCA Records), meeting our producer Ron Chancey, finding great songs, recording our first hit, "Y'all Come Back Saloon" (it released to radio in 1977), playing in Las Vegas with Roy Clark, opening shows for other Halsey acts like Mel Tillis and Freddy Fender, touring with Jimmy Dean (eating sausage and singing "Big John"), lots of TV, establishing a relationship with Harrah's in Reno and Lake Tahoe, as well as John Ascuaga's Nugget in Sparks, Nevada, performing at some huge showcases for fairs and colleges, performing with symphonies for the first time, and countless other career-building events.

But most of all we were finding ourselves musically. We were also slowly coming to the realization that we were now, finally, weaving our way out of the gray years and into the early days of visions turning into reality and dreams actually coming true. The Oak Ridge Boys were in the process of arriving!

Backing up "Hee Haw's" virtuoso showman (and our good friend) Roy Clark.

A DAY OFF IN RIGA

Leading up to World War II, Hitler's Nazi German army steamrollered over the Balkan States. After the Allies won the war, the tiny Balkans were given back over to what was then the Soviet Union and in 1976 the Oak Ridge Boys and Roy Clark found ourselves in the city of Riga, Latvia with a day off on the aforementioned cultural exchange tour of the U.S.S.R. in 1976.

We would see many sights behind the iron curtain that would change our lives forever and make us appreciate the freedoms that we enjoy in the good old U. S. of A. but this was a day that would stay with us forever. I can *not* talk about it without my eyes tearing up. Perhaps I can write about it.

During the German occupation of Riga there was a death camp built there, a children's death camp to be exact. During the Nazi's attempt to eradicate all Jews from the planet there were extermination camps built to do the job. What is left in places like Riga, Dachau, Bergen Belson, and Auschwitz are grim reminders of why our boys had to win that war. Thank God they did!

I had read many books about the death camps and I knew that the Riga ghetto had been the home of one Eric Rothman who became known as the "Butcher of Riga." In those days thousands of Jewish children were taken from their families, herded into trains and sent to Riga, Latvia. Here, they were murdered and their blood was sent to the front lines to aid the Nazi war effort. Rothman killed 30,000 people here, the majority of them children.

On this day off in January of 1976 we were given a list of things that we could do. The Russians always planned our day right up to the minute. We traveled only at night, we couldn't walk on our own, we were followed and monitored every step of the way by the Russian KGB. We had a few CIA guys around to guide us as well. As I stated before we were not allowed to sing Gospel songs and it really stuck in our craw. Roy Clark would rebel by singing "Just a Little Talk with Jesus" at any moment and at any time. In a hotel lobby, a street corner, a restaurant, boom, Roy would start belting it out.

"OHHHHHHH I ONCE WAS LOST IN SIN BUT JESUS TOOK ME IN."

We would join in of course. It is a small wonder that we didn't end up in a gulag!

So then. What to do today? A theater perhaps? A museum? A walk through the park? It was about one degree below unbearable.

"Is there a monument to the Riga death camp sir?" I asked our guide.

"Ya, der is dat! You want to go there?"

"Yes I do!" Everyone agreed.

At the entrance a very long sign reads, "Behind These Walls the Very Ground Is Crying." One actually enters this sacred ground by walking underneath this structure where the sign is and once on the other side, the temperature actually turned quite a bit warmer and the atmosphere seemed to thicken.

It was almost like we walked through an invisible shield of sheer emotion.

There was Roy, Jim Halsey, Kathy Gangwisch and Buck Trent, and the three girls from Roy's backup singing group, Sugah, and the four of us and our band at the time. B. James Lowry, Garland Craft, Mark Ellerbee and Don Breland as well as our sound guys, Skip Mitchell and Brad Harrison were there as well.

Everyone had this look on their face. There was a definite presence here and we could feel it. All that was ahead of us were the remains of several incinerators and buildings as well as pathways adorned with statues. Very beautiful tall structures that depicted human adults and children in various stages of suffering. It stared to snow. It was so quiet. So moving. The only discernible sound was a slight murmur beneath our feet.

The *ground* was crying!

We went into the remains of a building where children were kept in little rooms and there was writing on the walls in a child's hand. This one stuck out: "May There Always Be MOMMY, May There Always Be SUNSHINE, May There Always Be ME."

Every one of us wept. (I am weeping as I write this. I am not even certain why I felt this little trip should be included in this book but I am certain that God wants me to put it here.) This was a rare day. I have never had another like it. None of us has. There is evil in the world my friends and it is only our faith in God that can help us overcome it. We came face-to-face with the evil work that was done on these grounds not that very long ago; however, there was also a presence of peace that existed there as well. I felt that God had an angel or two on hand to let us know that these little ones were with Jesus now. I believe that they were also witnessing and teaching us. Do not forget what you are feeling. God has no part in the evil that man can do to man. God is love. Trust in the Lord and do your part to make sure that nothing like this ever happens again. Well, I still feel it now! Just as strongly as 28 years ago.

We all had pockets full of Clark Bars that we would have handed out to Russian kids from the stage and on the streets. It sounds strange but, everyone took out their Clark Bars and dropped them there by the wall of children's writing and then . . . we left.

Changed forever.

Red Square, Moscow

THE OAK RIDGE BOYS

"Shot in the Saloon": The cover for our first gigantic hit, "Y'all Come Back Saloon."

Recently on a trip back to Reno, I couldn't help but to reflect back on some of our earlier days in the Nevada desert.

First, Las Vegas:

We opened for Johnny Cash at the Hilton in 1973 and 1974 (as well as the Sahara Hotel in Tahoe)!

For several years after that, we headlined the "Country Music USA" show at the old Landmark Hotel. Jim Halsey

VIVA LAS VEGAS

The Oaks followed other southern

superstars in bringing their hot sound

to the desert.

used this stage as a showcase for the Oaks. He would bring in promoters and press from all over the country to see the group that he called "the future of country music," and a lot of good folks joined the Oaks' bandwagon at the Landmark.

We stayed at a real rat-trap called the Mansion Manor Motel during these bleak financial days and that part was hideous. But we were paying some bills at home and that mattered more than our comfort. Oh well, we weren't used to room service yet, anyway.

We opened for Roy Clark some at the Frontier Hotel during that same time, and continued to do that well into 1980, when we headlined the Frontier ourselves for the very first time!

Before 1980 came to an end, we signed a long-term contract with the MGM Grand Hotel and soon became a part of Las Vegas history!

Right up through the time we taped our TV show at the Las Vegas Hilton, the town has been a huge part of our history and success as a major, across the board, music act. Like Elvis, Wayne Newton, and others, Las Vegas has become a vital part of our lives as well as our history over all of these passing years.

Reno and Tahoe:

During many of those same gray and starving years of the middle seventies, it was Harrah's Reno that booked us to play for ten straight days in the Cabaret Room (a very fancy word for *lounge*).

We performed three 45-minute shows a night on a tiny little stage and, yes, we wore The Suits! Those brightly-colored Harvey Krantz suits that had even been to Russia.

Orange, green, white, and red.

We eventually added an all-white version and also a fancy denim version of The Suits (which were much easier on the eyes).

After the Harrah's Reno gig, we spent ten straight days singing in the Cabaret Room at Harrah's Lake Tahoe. We actually played this combination of gigs several times. These were, again, survival showcase-type gigs that the Godfather set up for us so we could pay some bills and *eat!*

Thankfully, not too many people saw us showcase in the Cabaret Room. These were some of the most trying and, yet, funniest times in our history.

The Cabaret stage was small! Very small, with a rounded front. There was a small clock, embedded in the floor, to remind each act exactly when to come off so they could then set up for the next act.

In Reno, we always had an alternating act and it was usually a bunch of drag queens. Yes, you heard that right. About ten semi-guys, dressed up as celebrity women like Cher, Dolly Parton, and Diana Ross, performed on the same stage.

We even got to know these fellows. Our dressing rooms were in a sub-basement, with a mysterious stairway that led up to the back of the stage. It was hilarious chatting and joking with guys dressed in robes and full make up.

Of course, we never stayed in a room at Harrah's back then. Our home away from home in Reno was the Lake Mill Lodge on the corner of, well, Lake and Mill.

This place made the Mansion Manor in Vegas look like the Monte Carlo. It was a dump (being kind)! The rooms were atrocious. The headboards on the beds were huge pieces of metal-flecked blue or orange Naugahyde. There were chairs to match.

Try to imagine multi-colored shag carpet. I believe the interior designers of this place were members of the Manson family! We even had vibrating beds. Remember those?

"Check in here — free TV and vibrating beds."

You put a quarter at a time in a little box and your bed shook. With the decor and the vibration, it seemed that you were either sleeping in an old, 1954 souped-up Ford, or deep within an old Peavey bass amp.

But you know what, friends and neighbors? We toughed it out! We sang our hearts out for every show and laughed until we cried most of the other times. We never headlined Harrah's Reno, but we went on to headline the main showroom at Harrah's Lake Tahoe for enough years to become legendary.

In Reno, we moved over to the suburb of Sparks, Nevada, where we headlined the main showroom at John Ascuaga's Nugget hotel. We still play there today.

In the early days of playing at the Nugget, our opening act was two elephants named Bertha and Teena. Again, you heard that right. Big elephants would do their thing for two shows a night – and many times would actually DO their thing right on the stage. (Even during dinner shows, *yuck!*)

"Now, ladies and gentleman, make welcome, the Oak Ridge Boys." Ha ha! Watch your step!

We really had some fun and made a lot of history in that wonderful, old showroom too. Bertha and Teena are gone now, but their memory is, uh, still there.

Here's a tidbit. We shot the cover of the *Y'all Come Back Saloon* album at the Bucket of Blood in Silver City, Nevada, just a few miles outside of Reno. We also shot the *Fancy Free* album cover in Reno, utilizing one of the Harrah's collection of classic cars.

This is a very small and limited look back at our important career moments in Nevada that Jim Halsey has used to help build and then maintain our longterm career. Jim has always believed that to be a major act, you must be able to perform in every kind of venue, from the county fair to the Vegas showroom to "The Tonight Show."

We have done all of that . . . and a whole lot more!

A funny little side story regarding The Suits! is that we were taping a television show in downtown Nashville and our suits were driven downtown in our old company station wagon. When we went out to retrieve our orange, green, white, and red Harvey Krantz suits, we found that they had been stolen.

The police came and filled out a report. About an hour later, the police showed up with The Suits! They had found them in a dumpster behind the Pizza Hut. Even the thieves didn't want them!

We brushed them off, put them on, and taped the TV show!

67

CASH, THE COWBOY AND THE GAMBLER

Over the years several music icons lent their expertise to help us advance our career. People like Johnny Cash, Jimmy Dean, and Kenny Rogers — good friends, good times, good memories.

68

I alluded to my Crossroads Theory in my narrative on Jim Halsey. Jim truly stands out as the most influential person to have ever entered the Oaks' career. But over the course of our long journey, we have arrived at many of these magical forks in the road. And God has certainly seen fit to bless us many times by placing some very special people in our way. Each would help to guide and direct us to another level of success. Only God knows what our lives would have been like without these men!

I have spoken about Paul Simon and Roy Clark, and of course, there are many more. Ron Chancey, Jim Foglesong, and most recently producer and friend Michael Sykes, just to name a few. But this little chapter concentrates on three magical stars who crossed our pathway and lit up our lives with the force of their immense talent, energies, and knowledge of the music business. Without these stones on the pile, our mountain may not have risen as high.

The "Man in Black," Johnny Cash came first and, to this very day, we love him dearly. From 1973 through 1975, he took us out on the road with him from time to time and paid us much more than we were worth, helping to keep our heads above water.

Working with Johnny, his wife June Carter, the Tennessee Three, as well as Mother Maybelle and the Carter Family gave us our first taste of what the really "big time" was all about.

Cash was a real legend. His very presence in a room exuded a magical and shimmering charisma that very few ever possess — a great songwriter, singer, writer, and actor. A big, *big* star with a heart of gold and a manner that suggested a wonderful and very distinct individuality, as well as a huge dose of pure American manhood, was John R. Cash. We learned a lot about life from being around him.

Johnny took us to Tahoe and Vegas for the first time. We would open with 20 minutes and then go off stage and sing some backup with him from behind

the curtain. At the finale of his show, we would join him onstage for a rollicking version of the old Gospel song, "The Fourth Man." We didn't have two coins to rub together in our pockets, yet here we were, singing with a legend on the stage of the Las Vegas Hilton. But it may have very well been offstage where he influenced us the most.

In the summer of 1974, our heads were hanging low and we wondered if we even had a future. We had very few dates in the book, and we were getting ourselves into debt by coming home from many trips with less money than we started out with.

The quartet dressed up for the 1985
Step on Out album cover.

One night, perhaps sensing that our spirits were a bit low, John invited us all up to the star suite of the Las Vegas Hilton for a late dinner after the show. Richard had been up there before with Elvis several years before, and he showed us where all the bullet holes were!

Johnny gave us a pep talk that would rival Knute Rockne or Vince Lombardi. He said, "Now, boys, there is magic in your group. All one has to do is stand here amongst you to feel this magic. If you give up, the rest of the world will never know what I know now. The Oak Ridge Boys are going to be big stars someday. So do *not* lose hope or faith in God . . . *or* each other." We left the suite that night believing in our hearts that we would make it. Johnny Cash had told us so!

In 1978, at the Country Music Association awards show broadcast live from the Grand Ol' Opry House in Nashville, Tennessee, on CBS Television, the Oaks were given the award for *Best Country Vocal Group*. The host of this show was none other than Johnny Cash.

The four Oak Ridge Boys ran to the stage but *not* to the acceptance speech podium. We ran to the host. We ran to the "Man in Black" and hugged him tightly. All he said was, "I told you!"

Johnny and June both went home to be with Jesus in 2003. Such a legacy. Such a loss. I trust that God will wrap them both in His everlasting arms and let them know how much they were loved while on this planet. They were among our oldest and dearest friends.

There are many others!

The first time we ever saw the old "Cowboy," Jimmy Dean, was at the Desert Inn in Las Vegas in 1975. We were headlining the Landmark Hotel, and we had a night off so we went over to see Jimmy. Besides, our Gospel friends, the Imperials, were singing with him on that show, and we really wanted to hear them as well.

We had no way of knowing that, off and on over the next three years, we would be standing up there where the Imperials now stood, singing "Big John" with a big star.

Jimmy Dean is a strong, tall man of the West, who became a big star by recording great hit songs and utilizing the medium of television to get the most out of those hits. His "Jimmy Dean" weekly show was a huge success and, much like Johnny Cash and Tennessee Ernie Ford, he brought the country and western way of life right into the living rooms of America. His homespun humor, music, and patriotism were loved by people of all ages, and his live show was always a lot of fun. Whenever we have been a part of his shows, or a part of his life, we have laughed a lot and learned a lot.

Dean was, and still is, the consummate professional. He works hard and expects everyone around him to work hard. He possessed a real love for the Oaks, and he always made us feel at home around him. He paid us well and taught us well, and we will always be thankful to him for his help and direction.

We would open the show onstage with him singing "Rocky Top." Then we would step back for a while and listen to his jokes. He was as much a standup comedian as a singer, and we would laugh until our sides hurt every night.

In the middle of his show, he would always say nice things about us and bring us forward to sing a few songs. Then we would all sing "Big John" and "America, the Beautiful," and the show would be over.

Usually, after a show we would go to his room and he would literally cook for us. Always some new sausage recipe that he had just created. Like Forrest Gump's shrimp, it was amazing how many ways the man

With music legends Dottie West, Ray Charles, and Kenny Rogers on a network television special.

could cook sausage. Of course, he made that pay off as well. More people today know him for Jimmy Dean sausage than for "Big John"!

Not long ago I was in a supermarket and my cell phone rang. The voice on the other end was J.D. telling me a loud and very funny joke. I found myself laughing out loud and as I looked up, there stood a life sized cardboard cutout of Jimmy Dean holding up and promoting his latest sausage. What a surreal moment that was. I hung up the phone, bought some Jimmy Dean sausage, and went home.

In 1977, when "Y'all Come Back Saloon" started to hit big, we would perform it on the shows we still had booked with Jimmy and the response was overwhelming. He called us together one night and said, "Well, you boys are on your way now. I'll miss having you on my shows, but I'll love you forever." The Oak Ridge Boys will always have a very special place in our hearts for Jimmy Dean as well. We love that old Cowboy!

The "Sweet Music Man," Kenny Rogers, taught us more about the music business than anyone, and working with him truly prepared us for the "big time"!

Kenny first invited us to do a few shows with him in 1978, and those shows were very successful. Then Kenny invited us to be a part of his big network TV special, which garnered huge ratings. Ray Charles was also on that show. Over the next year, the Oaks grew in popularity and so did Kenny Rogers. Ideas began to take shape for a big tour.

Kenny's long time manager Ken Kragen and our godfather, Jim Halsey, had meeting after meeting, hammering out the details of how to make this work and how to get a ton of mileage out of the proposed tour.

The Oaks were *the* hot young act in the business and were building a lot of momentum with hit after hit and a slew of awards. Kenny was riding high with songs like "Lucille" and "The Gambler," and his duets with Dottie West were also hitting big and winning awards.

So the plan came down as follows. A tour that would last one year and cover 90 cities. The stage would be round and would play in the middle of the arena. Dottie West would open with 25 minutes and then the Oak Ridge Boys would do 40. After intermission, Kenny would perform for an hour and during his set, Dottie would join him for a couple of duets.

It would be called the *Full House* tour and when it was all over, Kenny, Dottie, and the Oak Ridge Boys were a part of history. Up until that time no country music tour had ever been this ambitious or as successful, and for the Oaks, it was like taking a college course in success every single day.

Kenny Rogers is not only one of the classiest and talented men that we have ever come into contact with, but he is also one of the smartest. His shared insights into singing, touring, picking songs, and his music business acumen never fell on deaf ears around this bunch. We absorbed and learned from the "Sweet Music Man" every single day of the *Full House* tour. In so doing, were able to pave the way for our own big time tour that would come after "Elvira" hit it big.

We had all been big fans of Kenny Rogers and the First Edition years before, because they were one of the few pop acts in those days that utilized a big harmony sound. Songs like "Ruby, Don't Take Your Love to Town" and others were among our favorite songs, so it was a sheer joy to even be around Kenny Rogers in the first place. And he never let us down. Besides, this tour provided the Oaks with a wonderful opportunity to perform in front of a lot of people in 1979. To this day, long time fans of the group will say that they first heard us sing on the Kenny Rogers tour.

In 1984 and 1985, we toured some more with Kenny. We called it a reunion tour and it was very successful as well. We were still riding the wave of our big success of the early 80s, and Kenny was riding higher than ever with songs like "Lady." The amount of fun and success that we all shared together was mind boggling,

73

The Oaks have a very successful annual Christmas tour.

and we will love and respect Kenny Rogers for as long as God allows us to breathe air.

An interesting side note is that in 1987 and 1988, Kenny might have done more for us than ever before. He invited us, as well as a new kid named Garth Brooks to accompany him on his annual Christmas tour. Garth opened with 15 minutes. The Oaks followed with 30, and later Kenny performed a complete Christmas show. For the finale, the Oaks and Garth joined him onstage. The Oaks already had two successful Christmas albums and during Kenny's show each night a thought kept coming to mind, "Hey, we can do this."

So we began to discuss the possibilities of our own Christmas tour in 1989. Fifteen years later the Oak Ridge Boys are still doing our own big production Christmas tour. Every year is based on things we learned from Kenny Rogers. With the recent success of our *Inconvenient Christmas* album, television special, and tour, I would say we will still be doing a Christmas tour for many years to come.

So, here is a very special thank you from the Oak Ridge Boys to Cash, the "Cowboy," and the "Gambler" — Johnny Cash, Jimmy Dean and Kenny Rogers. One cannot imagine where we would be today without them!

Singing with Ray Charles at the CMA awards.

A FEW PIECES
MAY 18, 2003

Today we said goodbye to a saint. Valerie June Carter Cash would wave off such a description but it doesn't make it any less true; this was a very special woman. She will be severely missed by not only Johnny Cash and the rest of her loving family, but by all of us who existed on the periphery of her life.

June loved the Oak Ridge Boys, she called us her *babies*. Those *babies* sang "Loving God, Loving Each Other" at her funeral today while the Man in Black wept and waved to us. This memory will stay with us forever, much like that of a sturdier Johnny Cash sitting in the front row of another requiem years ago as the Oak Ridge Boys sang a Garland Craft song, "That's Just Like Jesus," to mark the passing of Mother Maybelle Carter, June's mother.

Some day, when the Great Choir gathers on that heavenly shore to sing for all eternity, a lot of old friends will come together once more, and I plan to be there, singing my heart out.

This is not the first time that I have said goodbye to a friend on my birthday. Our longtime bus driver, Harley Pinkerman, also left us five years ago on this date.

The funeral over, I headed out to my farm. This place has become my refuge over and over again for the last five years. I always feel close to God in this holler that rests on the Kentucky/Tennessee line.

So, *Little Joey* from Philly is now 55 years old. How about that!

I took a ride alone on my John Deere Gator just before dusk. I saw a momma turkey protecting her eight little fuzzy babies who were struggling to keep up with her. There was a beautiful doe, seemingly all alone. But I knew she was guarding a newborn fawn, so I went the other way so as not to disturb her.

Goldfinches and the summer tanagers flitted along the fencerows although it seemed early in the season for them. I parked a while by the creek and listened. Previous storms had swelled the stream and the sound of the rushing waters was very soothing.

Darkness fell, and as is usual for May, the night is filled with a kazillion lightning bugs blinking away as if they were a part of some fantasy movie. I almost expected a Hobbit to pop up and start talking to me.

Back at the cabin, I sat on the front porch and continued to take in the show. All of the barn swallows who share my home roost just above me, tolerating my presence, in nesting pairs, one sitting on her eggs and the other just outside on guard. I counted fourteen pairs of swallows in the eaves and could not help laughing as I realized how many more will be buzzing by my head next month. Come fall, before they decide to head off to Capistrano or elsewhere, there could be about 160 or so.

Inside, Mary had made a nice meal. On *ESPN*, the Phillies were even beating the Astros. Not bad.

Time to turn in, but first the message light on the phone was blinking. I realized that I had been out of touch on this birthday and that I had missed several calls:

My sister singing "Happy Birthday" at the top of her lungs (wonderful) . . . My daughter Jen singing it like *Elvis* (hysterical) . . . My daughter Sabrina and the grandkids singing "Happy Birthday to Pop Pop" . . . with a cha-cha beat (so sweet)!

And then a call from my friend, Duane Allen.

"Hey man, just wanted to tell you, that was one of the hardest things we ever had to do today, and I was so proud of all my singing

JUNE CARTER CASH

partners. I was honored to be an Oak. When Johnny wept during our song, I near lost it and I could tell you did, too. Looks like your birthday got a little lost today and I just wanted you to know how much I love you.

"Perhaps out there at the farm a few pieces will fall in place that will add up to a happy birthday. 'Good night, Yosef . . . see you at leaving time!' "

"Coming to bed, Hon?" Mary asked.

A few pieces had fallen in place, for sure. Goodnight, June Carter Cash. One of your *babies* had enjoyed a very happy birthday!

GLORY DAYS

The Oak Ridge Boys' stage show has always been dynamic, but the group was also a trendsetter when it came to production and technology. They were the first country act to use Vari-Lites, a totally wireless stage, a large scale point-source sound array, and as well, they broke new ground with a laser light show in their Las Vegas shows.

Chapter Eight

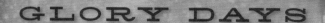

It is hard to explain the sheer energy of playing a major coliseum where every seat is sold and all ticket holders are on their feet screaming. The house lights go dim and the elaborate stage lighting truss begins to flash every color of the rainbow utilizing the highest technology of the day. Laser beams pierce the air and smoke rises up from stage in a cloud as the band begins to play. Then, with an explosion of pyrotechnic fireworks from each side of the stage, "the act" suddenly appears on stage and there is pandemonium in the audience as they begin to sing hit after hit.

The elaborate stage encompasses a walk around ramp so that the act can run up and over the drums, performing to the crowd that is seated behind the stage. There is also a platform on each side so that individual members can climb up and sing right into the faces of those who sit to the left and to the right.

Before the show, there were literally hundreds of people backstage to wade through — press, record label executives, radio disc jockeys from several stations, contest winners, local VIPs including politicians from both parties, friends of friends of friends who claim to know someone in the entourage, as well as TV crews from all the local TV stations wanting a sound bite from the act.

For the performers, hitting the stage is actually a relief, because they have dealt with a crowd most of the day. When the busses and semis pulled into town early that morning, there were several hundred people holding up welcome signs in the hotel parking lot. These folks had to be greeted before the performers could even get to their rooms and have some morning coffee. Then, more than likely, there would be an afternoon press conference, phone interviews, and a few big decisions to be made – and all that might take place long before sound check.

But, ah, that moment. Hitting that stage. What a rush. This is the stuff that dreams are made of. Little kids lie in the darkness of their rooms at night and wonder if something like this could ever happen to them. They sing in front of a mirror using a dust mop as a microphone stand – and a small oblong lampshade as a mike as they picture themselves singing on a stage like this. Big sound, lights swirling, people cheering, yelling, and lighting their lighters – holding them up high above their heads — all for you and your singing partners and brothers!

I could be describing the Rolling Stones, Bruce Springsteen, or Garth Brooks. But this narrative is all about the Oak Ridge Boys in the early 80s when for three straight years, be it a state fair or a major coliseum, we never performed to an empty seat. This was the *Cookin'* tour!

We were ready for this success. Touring with Kenny Rogers on the aforementioned 90-city *Full House* tour, as well as a plethora of big country hits and awards that resulted in five gold albums through 1980 certainly helped us build the vehicle that would carry us into the big time. But it was a little song called "Elvira" that propelled us to a level that existed way beyond our wildest imagination. "Elvira" was not only responsible for selling millions of records, but it took the Oak Ridge Boys from being a very successful country music act to becoming a household name. In 1981, everyone was singing "oom pah pah mau mau" with the Oaks.

Little kids loved the song. It was played at seventh-inning-stretch time from the local softball league to "Elvira" nights at minor league parks, on up to Wrigley Field. It was played during football games from

From the *Fancy Free* photo shoot.

With special guests: the Singing Senators
(from left: Jim Jeffords, Larry Craig, John
Ashcroft, and Trent Lott) and Charley Pride.

the county high school to UCLA, to the Minnesota Vikings. Every club band bass singer in every lounge in America was trying to sing like Richard Sterban.

High school and college marching bands were playing the song and its success was the talk of the town all across the country. This may not sound significant, but the underlying surge that hit us was because people knew we were the ones singing the song.

Several big TV appearances on shows like "The Tonight Show" and eventually our own HBO music special iced it for us. Jim Halsey made sure we got all of the mileage we could out of this song. I tell you that we could not go anywhere without people yelling "Elvira" at us and, in fact, they still do it today over 23 years later. "Elvira" was the kind of music phenomenon that only comes around once in a great while and it wasn't even a new song.

Dallas Frazier, who wrote the song (he took the name from a street in Madison, Tennessee), had a marginal hit with it in the early 60s, and it had been recorded before by several acts including Rodney Crowell and, ironically, Kenny Rogers and the First Edition.

A song-plugger for Acuff-Rose Music and a good friend of the Oaks named Ronnie Gant was in a bar in Texas and heard a house band sing the song. His wheels started to turn because he knew Acuff-Rose published the song. He thought of the Oaks immediately. The Boys had never cut anything like this and maybe it could provide something a bit different for them.

He came back to Nashville and gave the song and the idea to our producer Ron Chancey. Ron thought we should record it for the up and coming *Fancy Free* album, and he thought that I should sing the lead on the verses and that Richard should do the "oom pah pahs" all by himself.

The *Fancy Free*
album drove us
to new heights of
success. It was on
this record that
"Elvira" debuted.
She's been good to
us all these years,
and we love her!

From the album,
*Where the Fast
Lane Ends*

We recorded the song in one take and hit the road. It was January of 1981 and the Oak Ridge Boys were playing a string of dates in the Pacific Northwest. On an afternoon in Spokane, Washington, we ran "Elvira" with the band at sound check and decided to add it to the show that night. The Spokane Opera House was sold out, and we proceeded to rip through our hits of the day, "Saloon," "You're The One," "Sail Away," "Dream On," "Trying To Love Two Women," and so on.

I stopped it all down about halfway through and told the audience about our up-and-coming album on MCA. The band hit the intro to "Elvira" and we marched into history. The audience in Spokane reacted as if we had given each of them a condo in Montserratt. We had had a lot of success up to this point but this was incredible. We sang "Elvira" again. Then, we sang it again! We backed up and took a bow, and Duane and I looked at each other wide eyed. All the ACE said to me was, "Whoop."

It was a great moment.

We ran back to Nashville and told MCA to release this thing as the first single and they did. "Elvira" sold over a million singles and over a million albums over the next few months on just country airplay (unheard of in 1981). While "Elvira" was peaking on the country charts, the single (and title song), "Fancy Free," was released and became a huge hit as well. Then, "Elvira" crossed into the pop charts and continued to hit big for the entire summer and well into the fall.

In fact, right after Labor Day in 1981, we went to Anchorage, Alaska, for two big shows at the arena. A local pop station had just had an all-"Elvira" Labor Day weekend party, wherein they only played "Elvira" for 72 straight hours. When we got off the plane there were hundreds of folks there to greet us. After 72 straight hours of "Elvira," I was sure they were going to throw ice balls at us, but they didn't. We felt like the Beatles in 1964!

"Elvira" not only generated sales of over five million records, it won every music award given for excellence in 1981. CMA *Song of the Year*, ACM *Song of the Year*, a BMI award for the "most plays" ever, a

81

In Brussels at the Millennium Festival.

Billboard award for most airplay, a jukebox award for "most played," and a coveted NARAS Grammy Award for *Best Country Song*, just to name a few.

For the Oaks, our challenge was not to try to top "Elvira" but to at least record quality songs that would keep our momentum going. We failed with a recreation of the Fiesta's hit "So Fine" but scored big with "Bobbie Sue," "Thank God for Kids," and "American Made."

As I said, in 1981, 1982, and 1983, the Oak Ridge Boys never performed for an empty seat. Things would slow down a little over the next few years and beyond, but those three years of being the hottest act in the music business left a huge imprint on all four of us. It was a run for the history books, and we are thankful for the experience.

William Lee always feels like singin' all night.

Those were the real "glory days" when the Oak Ridge Boys were young and strong and ran with the wind at our backs and the sun shining on our face. Sometimes, today, when the concert hall is full and I see William Lee Golden take a knee to "thank God for grandkids, too," I can look back and easily visualize a sea of lighters in venues like Poplar Creek in Chicago or Pine Knob in Detroit.

When we start "Elvira" and I hear the big cheer, my mind's eye can still see the Summit in Houston or the Field House at Middle Tennessee University, with roaring louder than we are singing. And I can't help thinking of the Bob Seger song, "Like a Rock," and I wondered myself: *where did the years go?*

I wouldn't really want to go back there because I am very happy in my present day skin, but I am also here to tell you: "that Oak Ridge Boys' *Cookin'* tour sure did rock!"

THE "SINGIN' STEVE" YEARS

Prologue: We never believed that it could happen to us. We never would have thought that we could grow apart, but for a while there, we did. I don't need to write much about the parting of the ways in 1987, because it has been well documented.

84

Since we all got back together again in 1996, we have thrown these things into what has been called the "Sea of Forgetfulness." That certainly doesn't mean that we didn't learn some lessons. The lack of communication, understanding, and love that resulted in William Lee Golden leaving the Oaks was a heartbreaking and life-changing experience for all involved, and I am sorry to this day that I didn't do more to keep it from happening.

We could have all done a bit more, but things got a bit out of control and, like a divorce, the Oaks as well as some outside forces laid out a pathway. Somehow, like a train rolling on a downhill track out of control, there was no stopping or turning back.

This next narrative will pay tribute to Steve Sanders, as well as tell you how we all maintained and survived during this period. However, I will put my heart on the table here and tell you, I am sorry that we ever stretched our brotherhood and friendship to the breaking point from 1985 through 1987. I thank God everyday that William Lee Golden returned to us in 1996, and that we are now, once again, living and singing in harmony.

After the departure of William Lee Golden in March of 1987, the Oaks proceeded to keep the ship afloat for almost nine years, utilizing some new energy, a new band, some big hit records, and maintaining a big-time concert schedule that still included all of the major fairs and festivals, as well as prestigious venues like Caesar's Palace in Las Vegas and Universal Amphitheater in Los Angeles. Big tours with supporting up-and-coming acts like Randy Travis and the Judds also helped us to keep the momentum rolling.

Steve Sanders, a soulful singer, songwriter and former child actor who had been playing rhythm guitar in the Mighty Oaks Band for years, was asked to come up front and sing the baritone for the Oak Ridge Boys. He willingly took the job and brought a fresh new sound and a lot of experience to our stage.

85

He had played on Broadway (*The Yearling*), acted on TV ("Gunsmoke," "Playhouse 90"), and had even starred in a big movie with Michael Caine and Faye Dunaway (*Hurry Sundown*).

Steve's short movie career spawned a series of pranks that lasted for years. Every time there was a movie on television with a young boy in it we would tell our longtime bus driver Harley Pinkerman that it was Stevie. Even if it was from the thirties.

One night we were watching Clark Gable in the classic *It Happened One Night*. We told Harley that the little boy in the flick was Steve. Harley was nearly moved to tears over the fact that Steve had actually acted with the great Clark Gable. Not one of us ever had the heart to tell him that we were joking!

Harley passed away in 1999. He drove us many a mile for many a year and we loved him dearly.

Steve Sanders also had a huge career in Gospel music at a very young age. Billed as "Little Steve" Sanders, he sold more Gospel records as a young boy than people might ever have imagined. He had been a true child star in every way.

Old Gospel music fans would bring "Little Steve" records to our shows for him to sign. They would hold them up in the audience and wave them around. Steve would just shake his head and accept the ribbing that obviously came his way. But deep down, we all thought it was pretty cool because years ago we were also big fans of "Little Steve" Sanders.

Harley Pinkerman

Steve did a remarkable job with us in that he spent the whole nine years being known as "the new guy." That was tough on him; however, he always handled it very well because, deep in his heart, he always felt like he was, indeed, just filling in. Sometimes it was quite frustrating for him, although to his credit, he always gave every show all that he had. And I have always appreciated his hardworking showbiz attitude and loved his soulful voice.

He sang lead on songs like "Gonna Take a Lot of River," "Bridges and Walls," "No Matter How High," "Lucky Moon," and "Beyond Those Years." All of these were top-five records, with a few going to number one. We had some great success with our videos during this time as well.

During that same span of time, William Lee Golden still hit the road hard as well, touring with his sons, Rusty and Chris, who had put together a great band known as the Goldens. The Goldens would open the

During the video shooting of "Gonna Take a Lot of River." It marks the lead vocal debut of Steve Sanders.

show and William would come out later and sing. It was a really good show. I had seen them on several occasions, but I don't think William Lee ever knew I was out there.

The Goldens had some great hits songs and several cutting-edge videos. And William Lee also achieved a good measure of success with a high energy, great music show and some hit songs and videos of his own. His *Red Dirt Highway* was the number-one video on CMT for well over a month!

William has always had many great ideas and visions about how to express his own image and music, and he constantly made it pay off. Besides, as he has also said many times, "Throughout my years as an Oak Ridge Boy, I missed a lot of quality time with my sons. The years I spent on the road with them was one of my greatest blessings."

True-hearted fans of the Oaks went out to see both acts over the course of those years. Many of these friends were reminiscent of children of a divorced family, who spent a lot of time in their rooms praying that their parents would someday reunite but losing more hope with each passing year.

I will never deny that we didn't have our share of fun in those days. As always, "Boys will be Boys," and we always kept on singing and making the best of every situation. Unfortunately, having a good time became more and more of a chore as Stevie's personal problems edged themselves to the forefront.

Steve Sanders was a paradox. Along with his constant laughter and good-time spirit, he also seemed to possess a dark side. On occasion, he would seem to dig himself into a very deep hole, and he would start

We called him "Singin' Steve"
because the boy could really sing!

to feel like everyone was against him. The law, the system, his family, and every single one of us.

He believed that there was a constant conspiracy going on just under the reality radar screen that threatened to constantly undo him. These were hard times for us to endure and many times feelings were hurt deeply by the things that he would say while under this cloud.

I wish that we could have foreseen the future and urged him to get some medical attention for his paranoia, but that is now spilt milk and, to be honest, he would never have sought any help, anyway.

He told me once, many years ago, that all he ever really wanted to do in life was sail around the world and fish. And more than once I have believed that if William Lee and the rest of us would have just followed our hearts a little more closely through the middle 80s and communicated more love and understanding toward each other, instead of doubts and fears, perhaps we never would have parted ways, and "Singin' Steve" Sanders would be sailing and fishing right now somewhere off the coast of Madagascar. Perhaps I would get a phone call late one night from "Sailin' Steve" and hear him laugh.

After Steve took his own life at his home in Florida in June of 1998, I had three immediate thoughts.

I really loved him, perhaps not enough!

He must have been drinking or he would never have pulled that trigger! (He had been.)

I wish that he was sailing!

Folks enjoyed the Oaks with Steve Sanders because we still gave every ounce of ourselves on stage. The music was good, the songs were great, and we still maintained a good business sense that got us through close-to-nine years (which is longer than most acts ever last).

However, most of our fans knew it wasn't the same, and down deep in our hearts, I guess we did too. But, again, we all kept right on singing! William Lee Golden kept on singing as well.

November of 1995 would be a monumental time of change for the Oak Ridge Boys and, ultimately, for Golden as well. After some bitter problems rose up in his personal life, Stevie turned even darker. We tried to help, but it was very hard. All the things that Steve had imagined and feared now seemed to be actually happening to him. And no matter how hard we tried, he would *not* be helped.

"These are my problems and I'll fix them!" he would say.

One night in Fort Worth, Texas, he just removed all his stuff from the bus and left us high and dry with a date to play that night. He had scheduled an appearance on some national talk show the next morning, and

he insisted that this appearance was more important than us.

So, boom! Just like that, he was gone! He just disappeared into some Jerry Springer-like mist and I never even saw him again after that.

Duane Allen's incredibly talented son Dee was on a plane to Fort Worth immediately and arrived just in time to fill in that night, singing a private show in Texas for a machine parts company. Dee sang with us on through the middle of December, and then had to go home for his college final exams. That was a first for the Oaks. I think he passed, too, which was amazing because our schedule left very little time for hitting the books!

Former Exile lead singer Paul Martin filled in for the rest of the tour and then married Duane's daughter Jamie. (Paul played bass guitar in the band for years, and he and Jamie now have two wonderful sons.)

Through all of the time after Steve's abrupt departure, we were really not sure what to do. This was a career first for us. Total bewilderment. We spent a lot of time crying, praying, and wondering about the immediate future.

Perhaps it was all over. I had thought that it might have been over in 1985 or 1986. Perhaps, almost nine years later, we had done all that we could and it was now time to hang up the spurs. However, deep in my heart I think I knew that we would make it through this. It was just a very bleak and emotional time.

I called Jim Halsey late one night and said, "Godfather, these are tough times right now, would you please come out here and help us?" (I found out later that he had received the same exact call from Duane and Richard.)

Jim had been retired for a few years at this point, but he came out on the road to comfort us, bring some positive vibes, and bring us together. When he arrived at Bally's in Las Vegas, we all held hands as he prayed for guidance.

We talked about different ways to go. We could hire a young guy like Paul or Dee and change directions again.

Or, as someone casually mentioned, "Perhaps Golden would come back and sing."

That thought really lit up the room and brought several smiles.

I remember thinking that it would be a very cool thing for every wonderful reason in the world, but we all just left it lying there, because of the uncertainties (who knew if he would come back?) and many other unanswered questions.

Jim Halsey never pushed the issue any harder, which was hard for him not to do because the godfather had always believed that the Oak Ridge Boys were the four of us. But he left it all up to us.

Duane Allen and William Lee had patched up a lot of bad feelings years earlier. When Duane's daddy passed away, his final words to his son were, "Have you patched things up with Golden, son?"

Well, he did. Many times, Duane and William would get together, take a long drive through the country and chat. But I hadn't talked to Golden in years, and Richard hadn't talked to him much. I must say here that Duane took the first change back in 1987 very hard.

If you look at all of our pictures from the first year of the Steve era, including the *Heartbeat* cover, Duane is hiding part of his face. The sheer emotion over Golden's departure brought on a case of Bell's palsy, which deadened the nerves on one side of Duane's face.

There was more than one price to pay for all of us during that time, but this one left a mark for a while. The feelings now were much the same. There was just so much emotion and uncertainty about the future. We held hands, prayed again, and went home for Christmas.

The Oak Ridge Boys trio entered the Christmas holidays of 1995 with no real plan, but thanks to the godfather, we were feeling somewhat better.

Duane Allen called me one night and said, "Hey man, God has a plan. Maybe we need to just get out of His way and let Him handle it."

That sounded fine by me.

We were now leaving it all in God's hands and God was about to push me to Kroger's. I walked into the local supermarket with Mary's Christmas grocery list and ran right smack into William Lee Golden!

Welcome back, William Lee!

Epilogue:

He looked at me and said, "Joooeeeyyyy . . . "

Jooooeeeyyyy was shaking. It was great to see him. It felt good, but after the handshake and "Merry Christmas," I felt all empty inside.

I went home and called him. I didn't get more than three words out of my mouth when William said, "Come on over."

He opened the door of his beautiful home that has stood there like a rock and a beacon since 1786, and led me into his sitting room.

There was a huge fire in the fireplace. We hugged like old friends and our eyes watered. We talked about love and forgiveness and friendship. We reminisced about the "glory days," as well as the bleak days of our past together. And we also spoke frankly and honestly about mistakes made on both sides.

He sang me a few songs that he had just recorded. As I left, I told him, "William, I don't know if we can sing together again. I have a feeling that we can, but more importantly, thank you for your graciousness to me today. I will never forget it."

He hugged me again, and I cried all the way home. I talked to Richard, Duane, and the godfather on the phone that night, and everyone was so happy.

When we eventually gathered around a piano and sang together for the first time in almost nine years, it was like magic. It seemed that God was there in the room with us letting us know that this was right. Memory after memory filled our minds and hearts as we began to sing. All of the miles, all of the emotional ups and downs. We had been through it all. We had starved together, cried together, laughed together and moved mountains together. We had shared our dreams with each other and then lived out those dreams . . . one by one . . . together. And here we were again, singing our songs. Duane Allen called for a prayer and it was a beautiful spirit-filled moment. As we once again stood in a circle and held onto each others' hands, Duane asked our Lord for forgiveness of our shortcomings and asked for guidance and grace in the coming days and months and years. He prayed that we would always put God first in our lives and that we would give *Him* the honor and glory in all things. He also thanked God for our families and for good health and for bringing the four of us back together again. Then we sang "Amazing Grace."

Then we took it to the stage!

It was now New Year's Eve and we found ourselves in a very familiar place on a very familiar stage, Merriville, Indiana, at the famous Star Plaza theater. We had made a lot of history here over the years and tonight we would make a little more! First, we performed for about 45 minutes with Dee Allen and Paul Martin singing with us as they had been doing since Steve left. Then the stage darkened a bit and I told the audience that they were about to see the Oak Ridge Boys of the future. There was a full house of fine folks on hand. About 2,800 of our very best friends and fans from all over the country had gathered here to help us celebrate the coming new year. It was indeed a tremendous surprise for all of them when the lights came up and we introduced William Lee Golden. The response was staggering.

Golden entered stage left and joined us. As four, we walked together to the very front of the stage and the audience stood as one and applauded for ten straight minutes. I thought that they would never stop. It was one of the most amazing moments ever for

all of us. The band kicked off "One in a Million" and we began to sing. It was tough singing because all four of us were still weeping. What a show, what a night! *Golden was back.* We were once again the Mighty Oak Ridge Boys. Golden told me later, "It felt good to not only be singing in harmony again . . . but to be living in harmony!"

Now, almost ten years later, we are still singing together. God did indeed have a plan and, thankfully, our hearts were wide open to that plan. It felt so good that a certain godfather, named Jim Halsey, came out of retirement to manage and guide us once again (not that he ever really stopped doing that)!

I will always be thankful to "Singin' Steve" Sanders for stepping up to the plate and giving us nine great years. And I am saddened beyond words at his loss.

I am also thankful that we are still singing — the Oak Ridge Boys: Duane Allen, William Lee Golden, Joe Bonsall, and Richard Sterban. As it was . . . and as it is today.

This journey is all about faith in God, faith in each other, love and music, harmony and friendship . . . and it is all about, *forgiveness*!

New Year's Eve reunion in Merriville Indiana!

93

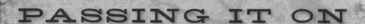

PASSING IT ON

There was a small little boy with bright blue eyes that had cerebral palsy. He could not walk or talk and was fed by a tube. When "Elvira" would come on the radio, he would kick and laugh.

Dear Oak Ridge Boys,
Thank you for those smiles!
– Mr. and Mrs. Lumpkin of Mississippi

P.S. He passed away at nine years old.

Chapter Ten

This note was handed to me by a man in the audience as we were taking our final bows after a Saturday night, rollicking good-time concert on the stage of the Grand Palace theater in Branson, Missouri. I had no idea what it said until I boarded the bus and began to change clothes.

We were already rolling out of the parking lot toward a date in Iowa when I finished reading the note. I stood there by my bunk, wearing just a pair of sweaty jeans and wept.

I gave the note to each of my partners. More tears were shed. The sheer emotion that bounced back at us from this little piece of paper caused us all to reflect upon the fact that not only are we very blessed, but sometimes you just never know or realize what an impact you might have on someone else's life.

The Oak Ridge Boys have always believed that as a music entity we have the choice of affecting people in one of three ways — positively, negatively, or not at all. Being Christian men with good roots and raising, we obviously go for the positive. If there is a way to give a little back and help someone along the way, we are usually standing in that line.

Children have always been the main focus of our charity work. We once put on a massive benefit concert in Dallas, Texas, called *Stars for Children*. The annual event lasted for five straight years, through the early 80s, and the outcome was very productive. The theme was child abuse prevention and awareness. We worked with many fine local business people as well as the National Exchange Club and the National Committee for the Prevention of Child Abuse. One result was the building of several SCAN (Suspected Child Abuse and Neglect) Centers in the state of Texas, which are active to this very day. Many friends joined with us each year at Reunion Arena,

Our greatest natural resource . . . children!

and we could have never succeeded without their help. Alabama, Eddie Rabbitt, the Commodores, and Roy Clark just to name a few.

We went on to become official spokesmen for the National Committee for the Prevention of Child Abuse (now called Prevent Child Abuse America), and the Oaks are still honorary members of the board. We applaud them for the wonderful work that they do year after year. No child should ever be abused and this cause has always been close to our heart.

Our song *Thank God for Kids*, written by Eddy Raven, has been used over and over since 1982 as a tool to remind people that our greatest natural resource is our children. We have also done a lot of work with Special Olympics over the years and have always taken a big role in the Children's Miracle Network and Jerry Lewis Muscular Dystrophy Telethon.

From 1982 through 1984, we were the official spokesmen for the Boys Scouts of America! We even played at a few Boy Scout jamborees over the years and recorded a few scouting songs. In June of 2001, at a celebration in Boston, Massachusetts, we were awarded the highest honor the Boy Scouts give, an award that is usually reserved for presidents and scholars, the *Silver Buffalo*. An incredible honor.

All of the Oaks are involved on some level, individually, with various causes and foundations that range from Make-a-Wish, to United Way, as well as humane treatment of animals, Native American issues, early education and literacy causes, and various veterans causes.

The Boys have also had the honor of working with the United States Department of Agriculture as spokesmen for their Take Pride in America program, in an effort to convince folks not to litter this great land. We even recorded a special song and video that has been played all over the country for years.

We have also worked with the United States Department of Transportation, as well as the Tennessee DOT, in helping to promote their Adopt-a-Highway programs and to encourage safe seat belt use.

The Oaks have helped to raise funds for various children's homes, hospitals, and orphanages as well as several National Sheriffs' Association Boys and Girls ranches across the South. We have worked closely with many local and state law enforcement agencies, as well as the FBI in an ongoing effort to influence young people not to drink and drive, or take drugs.

But our group charity of choice for over the past 20 years has been Feed the Children out of Oklahoma City, Oklahoma. Founded by Rev. Larry Jones and his wife Frances, this organization has done more to feed hungry children around the world — and here at home — than any other. We are honored to be associated with them year after year.

Kid-related causes have always been at the top of the Oaks' charity list.

"Thank God for grandkids, too!"

Through Feed the Children, we have built four Oak Ridge Boys' water wells in the Rift Valley of Kenya. How did this happen? Jim Halsey put together a big show in Nice, France, at the Acropolis Center in the spring of 1984. It was the grand opening of this grand and beautiful concert hall, and we performed there on American Music Night during a weeklong celebration. We decided to donate the proceeds of the event to Feed the Children, to be earmarked for the African water wells, and I am happy to report that entire villages have built up around each of those wells. Because, you see, where there is water, there is life!

We have also collected, literally, millions of pounds of food at food drops and concerts all over the country. Our Christmas television show in 2002 was done in association with Feed the Children, and because of the success of that show many hungry children in America saw a Feed the Children truck roll through their town. They received toys and, more importantly, food to eat at Christmastime.

Feed the Children truckloads of food run only because of generous folks just like you, so give them a call sometime at 1-800-627-4556, and if it is within your means to do so, please, help feed a hungry child.

There is a song from our first Christmas album that says, "When you give it away, it all comes back tenfold they say." Well, the words of that song are very true. The Oaks have always passed our success on to others and God has blessed us beyond our wildest dreams, but some of the biggest blessings received are in the example of the letter shared at the beginning of this chapter.

It has been downright amazing how many very special children have taken to us over the years. I could make a long list of experiences where our music has meant something on a heart and soul level to a child less fortunate. It could be Joey in North Carolina or Dawn in Memphis or one of hundreds of others. When a special child chooses to make the Oak Ridge Boys a part of their lives, or when our music has brought comfort to one of these special angels and their family, it has always moved us beyond words. It is blessing that cannot be explained. It is God . . . smiling on us.

(left) **Larry and Frances Jones,** co-founders of Feed the Children, distributing food to needy families. (below) **The Oaks** help out with one of their favorite organizations.

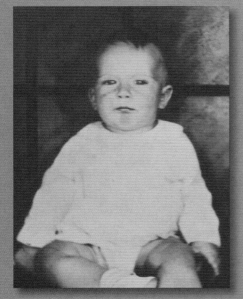

William Lee Golden was raised in Brewton, a small town in lower Alabama, near the Florida state line, in an area known for paper mills and cotton fields.

Luke and Ruth Golden reared their three children to work hard on the family farm. In the early years, they had no electricity, running water, telephone, or car. Social events centered on church.

Music was a special diversion for the Golden children, Lanette, William Lee, and Ronnie. After the chores were done, they would spend hours playing and singing. Older sister Lanette taught William to play the guitar, and for a number of years they performed duets on their Granddaddy Golden's local radio show.

"One really special song they did was 'I Saw The Light,'" Ruth Golden remembers. "William was pretty small when he first sang in church. He sang high tenor before his voice changed."

Ruth confides that she was probably more nervous than her children were when it came time for them to perform.

"I don't know that he got his musical talent from either one of us," she says, referring to herself and William Lee's dad. "One of William's uncles was a good singer."

In fact, that uncle led music in church, and William Lee's grandfather was a minister and played fiddle.

"All of our children really enjoyed singing, and all three were good at it. But William was the one who wanted it to be his career. It seems like I always understood that he would sing music for a living. He sang in school and in the FFA quartet. I wasn't surprised when he started talking about making singing a career.

"I have always been proud of him," she adds softly.

Ruth has difficulty picking a favorite song, but one song does stand out in her mind.

"I always enjoyed hearing him sing 'Sailing Toward Home,' " she recalls. Ruth says she also enjoys listening to the Oaks' newest Gospel album, *From the Heart.*

In November of 1978, the Boys would receive our first invitation to take part in the famous Macy's Thanksgiving Day Parade. How cool!

We had all watched this parade on television since childhood, and now we would get to march right down Broadway with all the huge floats, characters, bands, and Santa Claus. Most kids in New York believe that the Macy's Santa is the real Santa and all others are his helpers. Growing up in Philadelphia, your author always believed that the real Santa resided at Gimbels department store or at least that is what my mother told me. (The Macy's Santa can make a pretty strong case, and he did in the wonderful movie, *Miracle on 34th Street*).

On this day, we were having our own good time on 34th Street. We gathered in a celebrity holding area around 6 a.m. Then they herded us onto a bus, where we sat for a long time making jokes with Patrick Swayze and John Ritter. It was set up like a Branson tour bus with seats and a huge coffee urn and stocked with plenty of pastries.

Well, William Lee started pounding the coffee. We all did, but Golden really loves his coffee in the morning and really hit it hard. All of a sudden they gave us a five-minute call. We each took a turn in the bathroom in the back of the bus, except for Golden, who was still slugging down a last cup of Maxwell House.

We proceeded to board a huge float — the "Turkey Float." You see it every year, right near the front. The huge bird bows up and down and his tail feathers gyrate from side to side, and this year the four Oak Ridge Boys gathered in the front of the float where we would wave and lip-synch "Callin' Baton Rouge," as well as "Come On In" for the next two-and-a-half hours on what was to be known as one of the coldest Thanksgivings in New York City history! It was about 19 degrees with a very cold breeze, which brought the wind chill factor to somewhere around unbearable.

The Turkey Float no sooner got going, and Golden turned to us and asked, "Is there a bathroom on this thing? I have to really go!"

There is no need to go into details here. I will tell you that by some miracle, he DID make it to the end of the parade. We would appear in the Macy's Day Parade a few more times over the passing years, however, on this frigid morning in the Big Apple, riding the Turkey Float and pretending to sing in front of thousands of cheering fans and a live network TV audience was one of the funniest times that I can ever remember. I ached from laughter.

I don't recall that it was all that funny to William Lee Golden.

101

GOLDEN BOY

WHEN WILLIAM LEE GOLDEN SHOUTS FROM THE STAGE, "I FEEL LIKE SINGIN' ALL NIGHT," HE REALLY MEANS IT! THE SHOW NEVER ENDS FOR GOLDEN. *HE REALLY LOVES TO SING.*

KENNEBUNKPORT, MAINE: A MEMOIR

The lanky fellow running across the White House lawn just couldn't be the vice-president of the United States. Yet, he was! The Oaks were setting up for a show during President Reagan's first term. All of a sudden, George Herbert Walker Bush — war hero, business-man, congressman, CIA director, vice-president — was making song requests to the Oak Ridge Boys. Ever since, the group has been close to George and Barbara Bush and their lovely family. Truly, a uniquely American story!

102

Chapter Eleven

Prologue:

To really appreciate the following little diary, one must understand the relationship and amazing friendship between the Oak Ridge Boys and our former president and his wife, George and Barbara Bush. It all started in the fall of 1982 when the Oaks were invited by President Ronald Reagan to perform on the lawn of the White House for the annual con-gressional barbecue.

While doing our sound check in the late after-noon (a sound check on the lawn of the White House is not something that happens every day), a tall, lanky figure could be seen running toward us. A closer inspection revealed that the man who was smiling and waving at us was the vice president of the United States, George Herbert Walker Bush.

We had heard that "the Veep" was a country music fan, but this was incredible. He shook everyone's hand and gave us a vice-president tee shirt (very funny when you think about it), and asked us to sing "Freckles." He explained that he had to be off to Africa in a little while, and he could not attend the show that night. So we proceeded to give him a pri-vate show and answer his requests. We knew he was really a fan because he wanted to hear album cuts!

We have been singing for him ever since. On board *Air Force One*, on the campaign trail, overnight at the White House, command performance in the East Room (for the entire Cabinet), another congres-sional barbecue, as well as many times at Walker's Point in Kennebunkport.

We have been by his side on many other occa-sions, such as the Republican National Convention in New Orleans in 1988, and his inauguration at the Capitol in 1989. We joined him at the Summit on Volunteerism in Philadelphia in 1997, and at the Medal of Freedom awards ceremony in January of 1993. (Ronald Reagan was honored, it was very moving!)

President Bush has also allowed our whole family to join him in the Oval Office on occasion. (Our children will never forget it.) We have campaigned for his sons, Jeb in Florida and George W. in Texas, and they went on to become governor of each state.

We are proud and honored to say that we have also stood beside George W. Bush on many a campaign platform as he went on to win the presidency in 2000. We pray for him every single day as he leads this nation in these emotionally charged times. We will be on the trail with him once again in 2004, as he runs for a second term. In fact we have already made a few important campaign stops with "W" over the summer.

In June of 2004 we took part in a huge two-day birthday celebration for George H. W. Bush in Houston, Texas. It was called "41@80" (he was the 41st president and it was his 80th birthday) and many friends, entertainers, and world leaders all paid a wonderful tribute to our former president. We performed on the main stage during the gala and the next day after #41 jumped out of a perfectly built airplane with the Army Rangers at College Station, Texas, the Oaks performed a 45-minute set for the 5,000 people who had gathered to eat barbecue and watch the eternally youthful, former leader of the free world float on down to terra firma. It was really a wonderful couple of days, and we even got to meet Mikhail Gorbachev. He loved Richard's bass singing so much I thought he might import him back to Russia.

Yes, we love the Bush family deeply. America is a better place because of their service and we are better Americans, as well. We have been to Kennebunkport, Maine, just about every year and will go again in the fall of this year.

So here it is, just one weekend of memories with George and Barbara Bush — a Kennebunkport diary!

August 29, 1999

Late show in Alabama on the 28th. Bus arrives home just before dawn. Repack, pick up our wives and head for the airport.

Northwest Airlines: Nashville to Detroit, Detroit to Portland, ground transportation to Walker's Point in Kennebunkport, Maine.

The historic compound of our former president and adored first lady, George and Barbara Bush, where for the fourth time the Oak Ridge Boys and our lovely partners in life, Mary Ann, Norah Lee, Brenda, and Donna, behold the ultimate beauty of the Maine coast as invited guests of the Bush's. We all feel like giddy school kids with our hands in the peanut butter (just like we always do).

"You know where your rooms are; make yourselves at home," Barbara says as she hugs us all and kisses our cheeks.

With President and Mrs. Ronald Reagan after a performance at the White House.

The Oaks and wives visiting with their good friends, President and Mrs. George H.W. Bush, at the Bush's Kennebunkport home.

Within moments our former president pulls up in a golf cart, jumps off, and starts picking up our bags and hugging us at the same time.

"By golly, Barb and I are really glad you all are here."

By golly, he really means it.

Tide's out. All are gathered on the back deck watching the sea. The president treks all the way out on the rocks to his fishing spot. He is accompanied by me, Duane, and a secret service agent.

Fly fishing for sea bass. He stands on a rock, line flying through the air; the others look tiny back at the house, long way out here, special spikes on shoes. Big wave, totally covers the president and the Ace. They are head-to-toe in seawater, while leaving Joey dry. Scary for a moment, but doggone funny.

"That's enough; they're not biting anyway," says a saturated George Bush as we head back. He stops at least five times to point out little pools of colorful sea life among the low-tide crevices.

Snippet of a remembered conversation: Our president: "I worry sometimes about the apathy of the American public concerning overall politics."

Barbara: "Well, can you blame them? Look at what they are being put through. It is still well over a year before the election. Very hard on a mother, too."

Everyone laughs.

Windows open. Cool ocean breeze blows across the bed. The moon is high and lights up the North Atlantic to a silvery white.

August 30, 1999

Early morning gulls call out to get up. Duane knocks on the door.

"The president says we muster at the boat dock at 10:15 a.m., and breakfast is ready."

The day we met George Herbert Walker Bush (41).

A moment later, Golden knocks on the door and brings the same message. I won't hear from Richard. He is deep asleep.

Fidelity Two: The president's pride and joy anchored in a cove on the east side of the compound. Tourists line the road above and watch George Bush and the Oak Ridge Boys and Girls as we scream out of the harbor in this twin-engined Fountain speedboat, the ominous looking black secret service boat in hot pursuit.

Up the coast to Cape Porpoise to watch the seals, and then back up the Kennebunk River. The magic of a port town in Maine, although a bit touristy now (wonder why?). The old Maine is still there in the faces of the lobster men and their traps and boats.

"Hi ya theah George. . . . We miss ya, Mr. President!"

The president glides down the river and waves to all kinds of folks who are darn glad to see him.

A huge yacht is in port today belonging to some folks from Eli Lilly — the *Hilarium*. We dock and board the 115-foot craft and are gladly shown around. I am just about to freak out here. Now *this* is a *boat*.

Free afternoon. The Boys and their Girls walking all around downtown and shopping. A beautiful day. Richard has borrowed a bike from a secret service agent and is now pedaling for Nova Scotia! We run into Brenda and William. They tell us of a quaint little art gallery where the artist has painted beautiful water-colored renditions of Walker's Point. William shows us one, and we are off to buy our own.

"The Bushes are wonderful people," says the artist as she puts the pastel of Walker's Point in a bag.

"They are the best," says Mary with a smile.

Cocktail party at the house for all the Bush neighbors: No former cabinet members or senators this time around. Just some real good friends and neighbors. We sing for about 45 minutes, a cappella as we always do. Our biggest fan requesting his favorites. "Amazing Grace,"

Sailing away with an American legend — off the coast of Maine.

"American Family," "Feelin' Fine," and on and on. This is a wonderful and precious honor.

Motorcade: Okay, it is not like the old days when he was president heading from *Air Force One* to the White House, however, a motorcade it is. Secret service, the Bushes and us. We're not heading for a summit meeting with heads of state. Our destination is the Lobster Pot. The secret service does their job. All points are secure and in we all go. Thankfully, there is no danger lurking inside of the little restaurant. No bad vibes or threatening looks. Just wide-eyed tourists and patient locals who are all just a bit amazed that George and Barbara Bush and the Oak Ridge Boys and Girls are at a table eating lobster, laughing, and talking just like they are.

"I don't remember where the bathroom is here, do you?" says President Bush.

I jump up out of my seat. "In the service of my country sir, I will scout the area and return with a full report."

I disappear for a moment and return with a full report.

He is already on his way with a laugh and a salute.

"That was very well executed," he says. He knows my humor well after all these years, and I have a good handle on his, too. He can be a very funny man.

107

Walker's Point Vista, Kennebunkport, Maine by William Lee Golden, 24x36 acrylic on canvas, 2003

August 31, 1999

Breakfast with the Bushes, more walking, more shopping, a ride into town on *Fidelity Two* for lunch at Federal Jacks. He always takes us there.

Many stories are told. I relate how in 1980 in Monaco I screwed up by calling Her Royal Highness Princess Caroline "Your Majesty." A huge no-no.

"You could have never appointed me as ambassador to anywhere, sir," I said.

"And he didn't," said Norah Lee.

It was very funny.

"The Blues are running; let's go!" shouts our commander-in-chief. Three soldiers step up to the task. Duane Allen, Donna Sterban, and your writer. We stop near Walker's Point where some birds are "frenzy-ing," and Duane takes the time to pull in a beautiful sea bass. Then our president sets the GPS and points the *Fidelity Two* on a course toward Boone's Island Lighthouse, about twelve miles straight out to sea.

We roll at such a speed across the breakers that the secret service can barely keep up (but they do). Our faces looked like a fifties' outer space movie with the G-force thing happening. I think our hairlines receded another inch as we bounced and kicked across the sea, which looked like a polished white stone. But, ah, did we catch fish! Big Blues with big ugly teeth. Duane caught the most; however, we all pulled in a few.

Deep-sea fishing with the president is something that Duane Allen had always wanted to do, and he was very moved by the whole experience. After we got home it took a while to get our land legs back and to get our faces back to normal. George loves to drive that boat as fast as possible. It was so much fun.

A memory: The president says, "Joe would you look in that box and get my grappling pliers? I'm gonna need them."

Uh, oh. When I was little and my dad would ask me to get him a tool from the toolbox, it seemed like I never, ever, brought him the right tool.

What are grappling pliers? I panic just a bit, but this is a different day.

"Here you go, sir," as I proudly hand the correct tool to the former leader of the free world. It also helped that the said pliers were the only tool in the box.

Back deck: Jean Becker, the Bushes' executive assistant, brings us the final draft of George's new book based on letters, diary entries, and memoirs. We are mentioned in the book three times. I was privileged to read excerpts aloud. The book is then passed around and everyone reads. The work is incredible.

Yes, tears were shed by all in the salty air of Walker's Point. The ten of us, just sitting there eating sandwiches and reflecting upon the written words of a man who has been a war hero in the Pacific theater, ambassador to China, ambassador to the United Nations, head of the CIA, vice president and president of the United States. I love this man, and knowing him and Barbara has enriched my life and made me a better American. I know my partners share this feeling.

Dinner later at home: Just the ten of us again. What an honor. Barbara Bush asked us each about our parents. It was very moving as each spoke up about his mother and father. It was yet another memory that will never fade. One last night to sleep on the rugged Maine coast with the Atlantic breeze sharing our bed.

Learning the art of deep-sea fishing.

Standing proudly with President George W. Bush (43): Thank God for this bright light leading our nation through dark times.

The Oak Ridge Boys have performed at the White House several times.

Oaks performing at the "41@80" event.
Our 41st president had just jumped out
of an airplane!

September 1, 1999

George Bush took off before we did. He must speak in Chicago and then be off to open dove hunting season in Lexington, Kentucky.

Mrs. Bush saw us off with hugs and tears and "George W. for President" bumper stickers. The girls flew home and the Oaks hit the road again, meeting our bus in Pittsburgh for another six days of singing across the Northeast.

My Mary is home with the kitties, and I am at this moment in a Holiday Inn in Youngstown, Ohio, about to board the bus for a ride to Syracuse and the New York State Fair. In my heart I must tell you, I can still hear the North Atlantic pounding into the jagged, rocky coast of Walker's Point in Kennebunkport, Maine. I assure you, I will hear it for a long time. As long as I live.

THE ROAD

One night while the Judds were singing their hit song, "Girl's Night Out," we danced across the stage in drag. We had bought the women's clothes that afternoon at a consignment store. We were the ugliest looking women you have ever seen. Wynonna and Naomi came totally apart. It was a fun night.

112

Chapter Twelve

Another important element of our success is our willingness to hit the road year after year. Road life is what separates the men from the boys in this business. You do not have to love the road, but you really have to not mind it at all. If you are one of those who hates every minute of touring then, quite simply, as John Wayne said in the movie *The Shootist*, "Mister, you had better find yourself another line of work!"

A small town reporter once asked, "How can you do "The Tonight Show" and then come to a little town like Ogallala, Nebraska?"

The answer? Simple!

"The Oaks do 'The Tonight Show' so that we *can* come and play in Ogallala, Nebraska!"

Most of the livelihood of the Oak Ridge Boys comes from touring. Making records, doing TV, and talking to media are all a means to that one end. Hitting the road hard and taking our live show to America and beyond. A lifetime spent traveling up and down the highways is a big commitment that carries with it a huge sacrifice. I have said many times that I sing for free. I am paid to be away from home and away from my family. But for anything in life that is worthwhile, there is a price to be paid and a sacrifice made.

Success doesn't come with a gift certificate. It has to be earned every single day and for the Oak Ridge Boys, that means taking this show on the road. When young artists ask my advice as to how to make it in the music business, I always tell them that they must be *willing*! If the talent is there, it is only the beginning. Are you *willing*? Do you have the heart to do what it takes and make the sacrifice required to follow this dream? The Oak Ridge Boys, to a man, have always been willing!

Over the course of our long career, we have been willing to ride in cars pulling U-Haul trailers. We have stuffed ourselves into vans, trucks, campers,

and buses of all kinds. We have slept on floors and slept inside of truck stops and, yes, even slept in church basements.

We have survived car wrecks, bus wrecks, and fast-food chains. We stayed in some of the dumpiest hotel rooms in America long before we could ever afford to stay at a Radisson.

Actually, as I write these words, I am sitting inside a beautiful, Radisson hotel room overlooking the Mississippi River with room service on the way. These are better days for sure, but this *is* the Christmas season and being home *would* be better.

However, there is a big Oak Ridge Boys' Christmas show tonight in Davenport, Iowa. So, it is a simple equation. To sing in Davenport, one must *be* in Davenport. One must have traveled to get here on a plane or a private bus, and one must spend a good part of the day in a hotel room, waiting for that time to perform.

One calls home and makes sure that things are okay. One showers. One shaves. (Golden doesn't shave!) One fires up the laptop and checks e-mail. One does sit ups. One tries to make good productive use of one's day. Ah, but tonight we sing, and that is why we are here.

Life on the road is certainly not easy but what is? Building roads? Dentistry? Roofing? Duane Allen, Joe Bonsall, William Lee Golden and Richard Sterban have never pictured themselves as men fighting rush hour each day and spending each night in their bed at home. Music and singing have been our calling since day one, and that includes touring. I flunked geometry in high school, because instead of drawing trapezoids, I was drawing stage plots and little pictures of buses with four guys looking out of the windows.

We love to come home. It is always a wonderful thing to be home for a while. However, when it is time to gather at the office, park our car, load our gear, and climb aboard the bus, well, that is a wonderful thing, too! In fact, we

Radio interview during "Fan Fair"

feel blessed by God, and we are thankful that the opportunity is there for us to go somewhere and sing. As we always say, "We have bookings!"

This Oaks' hard work ethic has always existed, and it isn't about the money, either. Don't read me wrong. We have done well and we are all glad to be making a good living out here. It is nice to be able to pay your bills, but I remember times when we didn't have a cent and we still felt the same way. I didn't really start making a decent living by singing songs until I was 32 years old. I starved

throughout my 20s, while all of my friends and some of my family wondered when I was ever going to obtain a *real* job. This has been the case with each Oak. Each man was *willing*!

I remember when William Lee Golden and Duane Allen sacrificed paychecks so that others could be paid. I remember borrowing a ton of money, as a group and as individuals, to keep ourselves afloat, while we waited for something good to start happening. I remember March 3, 1974, when Duane, William, and Richard emptied their pockets of all that they had after a show in Wichita, Kansas. They gave their money to me to pay for a plane flight back to Nashville, so that I could be there for the birth of my daughter, Jennifer. I flew right back out of Tennessee the very next day and met the group in Montana. Then we celebrated my new fatherhood all across western Canada.

Although we approach our career with a keen and common business sense, I can honestly say that it sure wasn't the money that kept us on the road in those days, and it has never been just the money that has kept us together today. Touring and singing was — and is — our calling. It's what we do.

I might add here that years and years of touring have taught us how to balance things out as much as possible. I don't want you, the reader, to think that we are on the road *all* of the time. Many acts, especially rock acts go on tour once every several years, and that tour could last as long as a year and a half. Then, the act might lay low for several years.

The Oaks work all year long. The preferred schedule is three nights out, four nights home, followed by four nights out and three at home. There are times we go out for ten days to two weeks, and there are also times when we stay home for a few weeks. This is what works for us. It allows us to play about 160 dates a year and still maintain a decent balance of getting the job done and providing income for our people, while still getting in as much quality time with our family as is possible.

We have named our tour every year. I remember names like the *Have Arrived* tour, the aforementioned *Cookin'* tour, the *Hot Summer Nights* tour, the *Deliver* tour, etc. My favorite all-time tour name was the

115

Highways, Hotels and Late Night Pizza tour! These days we are on the *Red, White, and BluBlocker* tour!

But the fact is that many tour names are just promotional tools. the Oak Ridge Boys are really on the *Never Ending* tour and that suits us just fine!

A word about the songs — the Oaks also possess a love for the songs we sing.

As William Lee says, "Each song tells its own story and reminds us of a certain time in our lives when that song was recorded."

The Oaks have never minded singing our songs over and over and over again. Golden is right. I believe that songs mark time for all of us, and that is one of the great aspects of being men of music.

Don Henley of the Eagles once said that it takes an amazing capacity for repetition to endure a life of performing the same songs over and over again. That comes from a guy who has toured about four times in the last twenty years! He seemed burdened by the statement, but he makes a good and solid point.

The Oaks try to keep our show as fresh as possible each year. But as Henley articulates, we also have to possess that strong capacity for repetition (although it is certainly not a burden).

I have never gotten tired of singing our songs. Not once! Not even "Elvira," which we have performed more times than there are light years from the planet Earth to Nebula. Folks still want to hear the Boys sing "Elvira" and, to us, that is an honor. Therefore, no matter how many times we sing that song — or any other song for that matter – we always give the performance every ounce of energy that we possess. It just seems to come natural for us.

Another wonderful common thread is that all four Oaks are always in total agreement on this philosophy and, therefore, we just keep hitting the road and singing our songs. Check the tour schedule on our website, www.oakridgeboys.com. We are probably going to be appearing somewhere close to your house this very year. Come on out and see us! That ol' highway rolls on forever!

Boys Will Be Boys

The show has been over for hours. The big bus rolls down the interstate to the next town on the schedule. We are all fast asleep in our bunks. A misconception of the general public is that touring like this is very difficult. Hey, it is not home, but we actually spend a good percentage of our nights every year rolling along in our own little bunk with our curtain closed. We each have our own television with two different satellite feeds as well as CD players and books to read. We can even check the news and send and receive e-mail on our Blackberries . . . from our bunks! Imagine that! It is much better than flying. To fly, one has to get up early, change planes somewhere as there are very few direct flights to anywhere, carry stuff, check all the gear and instruments (a nightmare as well as very costly) Then, when we land, we have to pile into vans and limos and such. By the time we hit the stage that night we are already exhausted. Sometimes, the schedule calls for a fly date and they are always very well planned out and expedited. But for us? We prefer the bus! After a show we climb on board, change clothes, relax, unwind and eventually crawl into our bunks. When we awake, we are right there at the next hotel in the next town and we have all had a good night's sleep!

So, here I am, in a deep, humming bus sleep. Uh, oh! I have to go to the bathroom. There is an art form involved in climbing out of bed, walking down the aisle and going to the bathroom without totally waking up.

Our driver is pretty smooth. Billy makes sure that a middle-of-the-night walk to the bathroom doesn't feel like a train ride through the Alps.

Afterward, I amble back down the aisle in a certain, mindless stupor where my bunk awaits me. My special pillow, my eggshell mattress, my Philadelphia Eagles blanket. I go to jump in and in mid air (I am on a top bunk, always have been) my blood runs cold as a loud, mind-bending scream escapes from the core of my being. While I was in the bathroom, Duane Allen has silently crawled out of his bed and into mine. He has made himself as small as possible and at the right moment, in the semi-darkness he has jumped out at me while squealing like Howard Dean. Eeeeeeeeeeeeeyyyaaa!

My heart actually stopped beating! The Ace has done this to me for 31 years. Sometimes just once a year, or maybe twice. He always lets enough time go by for my guard to be let down on the matter. I will check my bunk before I ever crawl back in there again for at least a month. A long-term ramification prank if there ever was one.

Yes, Boys will be Boys!

STILL HOLDIN' ON

"When I go on stage, I get the same feeling I had the first time I sang with the Oak Ridge Boys. This is the only job I've ever wanted to have." – Duane Allen

118

Chapter Thirteen

Here we are, deep within the year of 2004, and it is still downright incredible that the Oak Ridge Boys are still moving full steam ahead. We are still singing our hearts out and still hitting the road hard.

Nothing has really changed except that we are all a bit older than we were before and, as William Lee sings every night, we are all "still holdin' on."

The Oak Ridge Boys work just as hard as we ever did and thoughts of retirement or even slowing down for an instant never seem to enter our thought pattern. I have heard Duane Allen say many times, "We have been able to plan out every aspect of our career except that we have never been able to formulate a plan to stop."

Many of our peers, like the Statler Brothers and Alabama, have reached the end of their line and retired. But not us! We don't even slow down, not even a little!

New music is still the key. It brings a constant, fresh approach and adds fuel to the fire that already simmers in each of us. In 2001, Spring Hill Music Group, our record label, gave the Oaks the opportunity to pay tribute to our Gospel music roots. For the first time in 30 years, we recorded and released a brand new Southern Gospel album called *From the Heart*. The project was not only nominated for a Grammy but won a Gospel Music Association Dove award for best *Country Gospel Album of the Year*. This honor came just a year after the GMA inducted the Oak Ridge Boys into the Gospel Music Hall of Fame.

In 2002, the Oaks recorded and released the critically acclaimed *Inconvenient Christmas* album for Spring Hill. Coupled with our "Inconvenient Christmas" TV special, which we did in cooperation with our friends at Feed the Children, and a 24-city *Inconvenient Christmas* tour, we literally steamrollered out of 2002 and on into 2003.

(left) *Yukon Autumn*, an original painting by William "Van Goghlden" (right).

We started the year on our new *Red, White, and BluBlocker* tour and also celebrated with a new studio album that pays tribute to American music in a very special way. Our *Colors* album on Spring Hill in 2003 reiterated to the world our commitment, as well as our devotion, to this great country we live in.

Only in the United States of America could we excel and live out our dreams each and every year of our lives. We love America, and we are thankful to the many men and woman who have sacrificed so very much of themselves so we can live in a free country today. We have never taken one day of living here in the U.S. of A. for granted. The music on *Colors* certainly reflects our heartfelt feelings and allows us to wax a bit patriotic.

Some of the events that have taken place over the last several years have caused us all to experience some anguish. There have been many disturbing events going on in the world. There has even been terror within our very shores. However, we get to look into the face and hearts of America almost every day, and we are thrilled to report that most people are positive, prayerful, and faithful about the future of our nation. Our constant prayer is that God will continue to bless America.

The songs about faith, family, hometown, flag, country, soldiers, and sacrifice have had a huge impact on all of us. The title song, "Colors," was nominated for a Grammy under the category of *Best Country Performance by a Duo or Group*. Such an honor!

We have released yet another new project this year for Spring Hill records called *The Journey*. It is an acoustic-driven and bluegrass-flavored CD that contains some of the finest and most poignant songs we have ever recorded. Utilizing more dobro, fiddle, mandolin, banjo, and upright bass than we have ever used before gives *The Journey* a different feel than anything we've ever done. It represents a whole new brand of excitement and creativity from the Oak Ridge Boys. Produced by Duane Allen and Michael Sykes, this project is so fresh and the songs so meaningful that most critics have called it an instant classic.

So it would seem that the Oak Ridge Boys are doing pretty well. Still holdin' on. In fact, we may be enjoying this group more than ever. The passing years and a bit of maturity have paid some wonderful dividends. Our friendship is stronger than ever and our love and respect for each other is at an all time high. Each man is very comfortable with himself and, at this point in our career, we really have nothing much to prove. So there is no real pressure. It is simply time to go somewhere and sing!

Like the mighty tree that gives us our name, each Oak has continued to grow stronger in many ways over these last several years. William Lee has become an incredible artist. Each day on the road he unloads his canvas, easel, and art supplies from a bin beneath the tour bus and sets up his studio in a hotel room — or at a nearby creek or pond — and he paints through the day. He has produced some incredible work, and it has really been fun to watch him grow in his love of art.

After a show, on a long bus ride through the night, you will usually find him reading a book on the subject or perhaps studying the great impressionists of long ago eras. Sometimes when everyone else is asleep in his bunk with his curtains closed, Golden is still sitting up front in the lounge with his head buried in a book about Van Gogh. In fact, sometimes I call him *Van Goghlden*! His work is indeed worthy. His colors are masterful, and he improves with each painting. One day soon, his paintings will be on display and his prestige as an artist will continue to grow. We are all very proud of him!

Duane Allen's energy for this group and the music we sing is never abated. He is a dynamo. He never stops working at keeping the Oaks' machine well oiled. He is usually the first one up in the morning, drinking coffee and talking on the cell phone to Jim Halsey – or the record label, or our press agent, or someone in our office. He is as tireless today as when I first met him well over 30 years ago. Along with Michael Sykes, Duane has co-produced our last four albums, *From the Heart*, *An Inconvenient Christmas*, *Colors*, and *The Journey*. With some great engineering and overdub help from David Ponder and Pete Greene, these last four albums are arguably some of our best work ever — and it has been the perseverance of the man we call the Ace that has made it all happen.

The Oaks have one of the most exciting shows on the road.

Richard Sterban takes more of a leadership role in our business every year. As I mentioned earlier, his conservative nature and his even keeled decision making has helped the Oak Ridge Boys to enjoy a good balance of keeping a big show on the road, yet still being very cost conscious.

Richard keeps an eye on the bottom line and makes sure that we are well anchored. He takes on the majority of press interviews that come our way, and there are many. Sometimes, Richard will do as many as five phone interviews just to help promote one date.

We call them *phoners*, and we all do some of these. But Richard usually takes on the lion's share. His representation of the group on radio and in newspapers articles is always first class. His sheer enthusiasm for the group never wavers.

Most people don't know that Richard is also an amateur meteorologist; therefore, we always know what the weather will be like in any given town we are passing through.

He is still my best friend.

As for me, Joseph S. Bonsall, besides my constant devotion and contribution to the Oaks, I have been writing for years. Along with writing many articles for the Internet and country and Gospel magazines and periodicals, my first books were the very popular *Molly The Cat* book series. *Molly*, *The Home*, *Outside*, and *Brewster* were released from 1997 to 1999. The series was published by Ideals Children's Books and illustrated beautifully by Erin Marie Mauterer.

I have also written an inspirational biography, published by New Leaf Press, and based on the lives of my own parents. *G.I. Joe and Lillie* has been very successful. I hope you have read it.

I have also co-authored a book inspired by our song, "The Most Inconvenient Christmas." *An Inconvenient Christmas* will be published by New Leaf Press in 2004.

I am, in point of fact, sitting in the back of the bus right now with my laptop booted up and running hot, deep in the process of writing this very book that you are holding in your hands!

Duane working with the troops for Feed the Children.

I am also learning to play the banjo. My old friends from Philadelphia will be shocked over that revelation. *Ban-Joey*! It boggles the mind!

On more than one occasion I have heard each of us say, "If God continues to bless us with good health, we can keep on singing."

This is very true. One of the main reasons for our longevity and success to this point is good health. In all honesty, there are a lot of hard miles on these engines.

We have all lost a few friends and loved ones over the last several years. Many have departed from this world way too soon. Their departures provide us with a good barometer, which indicates how very fragile our lives can be. But keeping that in mind, we all try real hard to do the right things for our body.

I will not say that we are all totally health conscious, but I can say that we do take pretty good care of ourselves. Duane lifts weights and works out with a trainer and has changed his diet dramatically over the years.

Richard has always eaten right, and he rides a bicycle twenty miles or more every day if the weather is right and the opportunity is there. His bike is always in a bay beneath the bus right beside William's art gear.

William Lee and I are both walkers, and I mean we can walk a long, long way. William has been a long distance walker for as long as I have known him. I used to run and play a lot of tennis but the joints won't take the running anymore, and for some reason my racket is a bit rusty. I guess I should pick it back up! I also work pretty hard on my farm on my off days and that definitely burns up a few calories.

We all try our very best to get in a good night's sleep, which is extremely important. We

I once ran into a man backstage at the Strawberry Festival in Plant City, Florida, who was 96 years old. He looked great, and he said he felt great.

"The key, young man," he said, "is good health. You can be 20 years old and if your health is bad, you just cannot excel at all in living a good life. All of my friends and family caught a good dose of bad health along their journey. A heart attack here, a cancer bout there, but me? I am as healthy as a horse. Always have been. I am all alone now, but God has been good to me."

I have never forgotten this man or his words.

We have a very special friend who just turned 104 years old. She is Aunt Una Reeks from Virginia. She has been coming to see us since she was a young girl of 78 when she lied to a security guard backstage at Busch Gardens in Williamsburg. She told him that she was our drummer's "Aunt Una," and she followed that little white lie right into our dressing room! She has been our number one "groupie" ever since! God has blessed her with good health. Aunt Una has inspired us for decades. She just might live to be 120!

also laugh a lot, and I think that is good for you as well. We try to stay in shape for our own personal reasons and it is a viable display of good common sense to do so. But there is more to it than that. When we hit that stage at night we want to be good. We want to possess the energy to give people their hard-earned money's worth, and a bunch of out-of-breath old guys just doesn't cut it.

Call it pride if you will, but the philosophy works for us. Our tank feels full at night on stage even when we are tired or running a bit on empty. Being somewhat conditioned and in reasonably good shape helps this cause. Besides, it feels great to run across that stage and sing "Dancin' the Night Away" and still have enough energy left to run up a mountain and back. It always has!

The bottom line? Like that wonderful old man in Florida, and like our dear Aunt Una, so far God has blessed us with good health. For this we are very, very thankful.

As I said in my opening thoughts, quoting the Bill and Gloria Gaither song, "Loving God, Loving Each Other." This story never really ends. It certainly doesn't end with this book. The words "the end" will *not* appear here. There is never really a final song. There are many more miles to go and many more songs to sing for the army of four that you know as the Oak Ridge Boys.

So, bring on the future. We are ready to take on whatever challenge God has in store for us, and we thank each of you out there who has cared enough about us to take us into your home and into your lives. It is for YOU that we exist.

God bless you one and all.

Joseph S. Bonsall

Richard carries a bicycle on the bus, and Duane hits during an ORBITS game.

127

A Mother's Perspective

Duane Allen's parents, Loretta and Fred Sr., raised six children near the small town of Taylortown, Texas. They were farmers who enjoyed music as a pastime. The family sang together at home and at church.

Duane, the youngest, "was exposed to gospel music and harmony singing from the time he was born . . . and he always enjoyed it. We used to have to stand him on a box when he was so young, so he could see over the podium," says Loretta.

One of her fondest memories of Duane's singing when he was a child is "when he was four or five years old, before he could read, and he would lead the congregation in a selection from the church hymnal — holding the hymnal upside down with his right hand, while he directed with his left hand!"

Loretta says her favorite Oak Ridge Boys song is "Sail Away," and the song that she has enjoyed hearing Duane sing since childhood is "My God Is Real."

"We were thrilled that he wanted to be a professional singer, we knew he had the talent. We live in a small community, and folks around recognized that his voice was special."

When he graduated from East Texas State University with a degree in music, he went home for one night's sleep and announced that he was heading to Nashville.

Even more than his accomplishments, Loretta says she is proud of her son's character. She feels that his work with schools and the underprivileged, both personally and through the Oak Ridge Boys, is in keeping with his raising.

At first glance one might think Duane Allen a tad compulsive. His constant energy level for creativity, progress and improvement, as well as his daily work ethic and common sense approach to things, can become easily thrown way off course by small thinking, mediocrity or negativity.

The Ace exists on a plane that seeks to rise up above the nonsense and get the job done. In this atmosphere of constant demand and pressure, it takes real understanding and fortitude to be able to weed through the gray areas and come up with viable answers and solutions. If that is being a bit compulsive, then so be it. But, if I were in deep trouble and needed immediate help, the first person I would call is Duane Allen. Why? Because he would be by my side in a heartbeat, leading the way through the darkness before most people would have even realized the lights were out. If being compulsive means getting the job done and getting it done right, while at the same time caring for your brothers and friends and family and fellow workers at the highest level, then Duane Allen is the one that you choose first when your hand reaches the top of the bat.

OUR ACE PRODUCER

NO ONE WORKS HARDER AT KEEPING THE OAKS

AFLOAT THAN DUANE ALLEN. HE IS ON A CONSTANT,

EVERYDAY MISSION TO KEEP THINGS GOING IN GOOD BUSINESS

FASHION, AS WELL AS KEEP US FRESH IN A CREATIVE WAY.

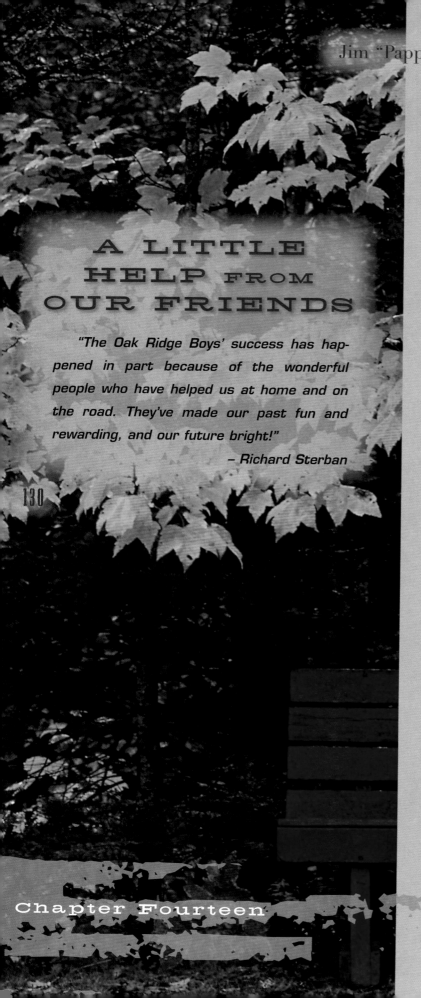

A LITTLE HELP FROM OUR FRIENDS

"The Oak Ridge Boys' success has happened in part because of the wonderful people who have helped us at home and on the road. They've made our past fun and rewarding, and our future bright!"

– Richard Sterban

Chapter Fourteen

Jim "Pappy" Glass drove our tour bus for six years and retired recently. Before him, the one-and-only Harley Pinkerman drove us for two decades before he lost a battle with cancer in 1998. Both of these men were old tour bus-driving legends who delivered the Oak Ridge Boys safely to a multitude of performance venues and back home again time after time, year after year.

The mantle or, should I say, the steering wheel has now been passed over to Billy Smith, who is already known as one of Nashville's top tour bus drivers, and we are honored to have him here. He, likewise, is thrilled to be working for the Oaks, a good, steady, consistent job that pays well and even provides health insurance. A workplace that is chock full of good people who actually care about what they are doing.

It is impossible to overstate our appreciation to those behind-the-scenes people who have worked for us for so many years. These are the ones who keep the Oak Ridge Boys' machine rolling, and in this little chapter, I am going to attempt to pay a tribute to our management, staff, crew, and band, without whom we would not exist on any level.

One cannot build a house without a good foundation — or an arch without a keystone — and our hard working people are indeed the true force behind our longtime career. As stated earlier, nothing just happens. It takes a team of hard-working people who toil daily in the trenches and make sure that every detail is in order.

Some of these folks have just been with us a short time and others have been with us for a very long haul. Let's meet them all.

ORB, Inc. Management and Staff

Jon Mir: Jon has been with us for 31 years. He is our operations manager as well as production manager and member of our in-house Operations Management Team. Jon oversees all communication

131

Ryan Pierce

between the William Morris Agency (Paul Moore) and the Oaks and coordinates our complete tour schedule as well as television appearances, working closely with Jim Halsey. He fronts all of the dates from a production and contractual standpoint.

He is our resident techno wiz kid and is the webmaster of our website, www.oakridgeboys.com. In what little spare time he has left, he designs and operates websites through his Moving Pixels company, including the web site of your author, www.josephsbonsall.com.

Here are some words from Jon Mir: "I was interviewed for my first position with Superior Sound Studios (owned by Duane Allen), engineering the radio show 'Gospel Country,' on December 30, 1973. I spent the next two years doing that and engineering recordings at Superior. During that period, I also traveled some with the Oaks doing Gospel shows around the country.

"In 1977, I went on the road as house soundman. I was still in college at the time and would come in off a trip and hit the classes. When the 'Elvira' days came along, I continued mixing house sound but added the hat of production manager.

"In those days we had the largest tour on the road, with three semis and three buses. We also set a lot of firsts, like being the first to use wireless microphones and instruments, walkie-talkies for production personnel, first in country music to use moving lights (Vari-Lites), and the first country band to use lasers in Vegas productions, to name a few.

"In 1986, I was named to the Operations Management Team, which is where I reside today — 2004. I still wear the production manager's hat, even though I do not mix shows anymore. During my tenure, I have worn a lot of part-time hats as well — computer guru, webmaster, photographer, videographer, editor, bus driver, truck loader, and 'chief cook and bottle washer' as Joe says."

Timmer Ground: "Captain Irish," road manager supreme. Rides with the Boys and is totally responsible for getting the whole entourage from point A to B to C on a daily basis. He coordinates all aspects of the road including overseeing drivers, bus leasing, trucking deals, hotel rooms, flights, meet and greets, special requests, backstage access, leaving times, arriving times, catering, and more.

He is in daily close contact with promoters, travel agents, and radio stations. He is a tireless warrior who has worked with us for 23 years. Perhaps his most important function is to make sure that the Direct TV satellite dish is in working order!

Ryan and Donnie

Timmer and Joe

A word from the Captain: "In 1979, I saw two of the sharpest buses pass me at a high rate of speed. The CB radios were buzzing about the Oak Ridge Boys. Not long after that I was riding on one of those buses at a high rate of speed.

It has been a true honor to work for these guys. A lot of people cannot say that their employers are their true friends.

"I've met presidents and sports figures and the list goes on and on. And here it is 2004 and it seems time has flown as fast as those buses did. God bless the Oak Ridge Boys!"

(As this book goes to print Timmer has decided to retire from the road and go into the bus leasing business. He is a good friend and we thank him for all the years that he has given us. We wish him well. Our new road manager is a big ol' Mississippi boy named Todd Brewer. He has a ton of experience and possess a heart of pure gold. We love him already!)

Todd Brewer

Karin Warf: She is our bookkeeper, records manager, and controller for the company. She is part of the OMT (Operations Management Team). All ORB business comes through her door! She maintains files on all concert venues; handles ticket requests, payroll, and employee files; coordinates insurance; and maintains contact with accountants, lawyers, personal management, and booking agency offices. She has been the backbone of our office for 34 years.

Erma Smith: Her friendly voice answers the phone most of the time and she is also an assistant to Karin. She expedites most of the paying of the bills and she also coordinates travel arrangements with the ORB travel agency and our road manager. She compiles a weekly trip sheet that is faxed, e-mailed, and snail-mailed to each employee and family member. Give her a call sometime. Erma usually has the answer. She has been here for about 30 years.

Kathy Harris: She is the head of marketing, promotions, and image — as well as a member of our Operations Management Team — and is a positive force behind our decision-making process.

Kathy liaisons between the four Oaks and anyone who needs an answer on any variety of subjects: records labels, Jim Halsey, producers, songwriters, politicians, and friends from all walks of life. She also works closely with Sandy Brokaw, our publicist.

Kathy has been an "Oak Ridge Girl" for 31 years. A few words from her:

"Right after college graduation, I was blessed to find a place in the Oaks' organization. It was a 'ground floor' opportunity for a kid from southern Illinois and fulfilled my dream of working in the Nashville music industry.

133

Jimmy Fulbright

"The Oaks soon became an internationally acclaimed music group, and as they achieved more and more success, I was given the chance to grow toward the creative end of the business! Oak Ridge Boys, Inc. has set many precedents in the 'business of music,' and I'm proud to have been a part of such history!

"While based in the office, I've also spent a lot of time on the road during the past three decades — handling photo shoots, video shoots, press events, and other special projects. Through the years, my job has included everything from industry relations to public relations, art direction to graphic design, tour-sponsorship coordination to administration, and now, book agent!

"There are many projects which stand out as especially memorable or fulfilling. High on that list is our charity work with Stars for Children; the opening of the Acropolis in Nice, France; the Radio City Music Hall concert; publishing projects, which include tour books, the Oaks' *Our Story*, and Joe's *G.I. Joe & Lillie*; and helping produce the George and Barbara Bush 5oth wedding anniversary charity fundraiser."

Linda Kirkpatrick: Linda works as assistant to Kathy in marketing and promotion. She also handles all fan club responsibilities, including putting together our annual fan club open house, as well as newsletters, mail-outs, fan mail, in-house merchandising, and shipping management. Linda excels in new product development as well as community relations. She has been a friend to the fans of the Oak Ridge Boys for over 20 years!

Jim Halsey: Exclusive management since 1975, Jim Halsey, Impresario.

Legal Counsel

S. Gary Spicer: He has represented and advised the Oaks on all legal matters pertaining to business and taxes since 1984. He is an honest and sincere man with a heart of pure gold and our lives are constantly enriched by his friendship and common sense.

Gary also represents many major league ballplayers and big business names. He also represents and provides counsel for several of us individually.

"Is that you, counselor?"

William Coben: William Coben acted as our music business attorney from 1975 - 2003. He was responsible for hammering out all of the legalities of our recording contracts.

Booking

Paul Moore: Paul is the agent in charge of the Oak Ridge Boys at the William Morris Agency, the most respected booking agency in America.

This man, as well as his associates, **Rick Shipp, Gayle Holcomb, Barry Jeffrey,** and **Rob Beckham** are responsible for negotiating and finalizing each and every contracted date that the Oaks agree to play. Offers for fairs, festivals, theaters, or even a gas station opening all come across the desk of Paul Moore. He and Jon

Mir work closely in coordinating each and every date so it makes sense logistically, as well as financially. He is a good man and a good friend. We love him dearly. Paul Moore has been a major cog in our wheel for 14 years.

Press and Publicity

Sanford Brokaw of the Brokaw Company: Publicity and how the press is handled are vital to the career of a music act and the Oaks are fortunate to have the best in the business. When Kathy Gangwisch, our longtime publicist, and her assistant Beckie Collins, retired a few years ago we enlisted the help and service of our good friend, Sandy Brokaw.

All ORB press and publicity is handled by Sandy. In fact, when Kathy Gangwisch first joined us in 1975, she was part of the Brokaw Company.

Sandy is a legend and a friend. He can get you in *USA Today* and even better, he knows more about baseball than anyone on the planet! Sandy has represented us full-time for the past four years.

The Crew

Jeffrey Douglas: is our stage manager, guitar and keyboard tech. He coordinates all load-ins and load-outs. The ultimate roadie, Jeff can do anything from building a house to building a guitar — from scratch.

Musicians from all over the country send their guitars to Jeff for repair and maintenance. He also plays some incredible rhythm guitar with the band, offstage, on most of our songs, which really adds to the overall sound. Jeff has been here for ten years.

135

The "Panther," "Synge," the "Big Guy," and "Guitar" (Jimmy Fulbright, Ronnie Fairchild, Chris Golden, Donnie Carr)

Chris Golden

Dave Boots: He's the lighting director supreme, as well as assistant stage manager.

Dave makes any stage look great from a performing arts center to a county fair. He is a very talented guy. He also helps Mike sell ORB merchandise at most shows. He has been with us for ten years. Light us up, Boots!

Marko Hunt: A longtime friend and soundman, Marko has been twisting knobs for the Oaks for 24 years. His long-term dedication, talent, and caring attitude have paid dividends to Oaks' audiences throughout the years. He is the one who mixes the sound out front with an expert set of ears. Not too loud, not too soft — a perfect mix, always. Sounds good, Marko!

Cliff Hall: He is monitor sound-mixer for the Oaks and band. Cliff makes sure that the sound in our ears and speakers onstage is just right so that we can concentrate on performing. He is the best ear man that we have ever had. He has been our stage sound-mixer for four years. We really appreciate Clifton.

Mike Campbell: All merchandising sales go through "Sweet Mikey C." He meets and greets folks with a special Texan charm. Always friendly and helpful, he will sell you a book, a tee shirt or CD and make you glad that you spent your hard-earned money with him at the "merch" table. Say "hello" to Mike at a show. You will like him a lot. He has been here selling swag for seven years.

Bus Drivers

A tough and responsible job, the bus driver maintains the bus, keeps it clean, keeps the food pantries stocked with goodies, and most importantly, gets the Boys, band, and crew to the gig and home smoothly and safely.

Billy Smith, Jr. drives the Boys' bus and **Billy Smith, Sr.** drives the band and crew. Pray for them as they are always driving somewhere down a long and dark highway carrying a sleeping bunch of fathers and grandfathers to another corner of America.

Truck Driver

Jerry Pope drives the big eighteen-wheeler rig for the Oaks. His job is one of the hardest. He travels alone on most nights, moving our gear from place to place. And he is always there before us, on time.

Jerry Pope is one of the best-known show bus drivers in the business. Many times when we have a few days off the road and we are home with our loved ones, Jerry is still out there moving our stuff down a highway. You really can't miss that huge *Red, White, and BluBlocker* Oak Ridge Boys' truck. If you should see it, give a wave to Jerry and send up a little prayer for his safety.

The Mighty Oaks Band

Ron Fairchild: Quite possibly the greatest musician on the planet. He has been our "Master of the Keyboards" for almost 25 years. He is a master of any other instrument he picks up as well.

Ronnie's dad, Tommy Fairchild, played piano for the Oak Ridge Boys in the late 50s throughout most of the 60s. It just wouldn't be the Oaks without Ronnie on keyboards.

Don "Guitar" Carr: Our young virtuoso has played the creative and driving lead and rhythm guitar for the Oak for 12 years. He is a stage force to be reckoned with and one of the nicest guys that one would ever want to meet. He is a positive life force and a tremendous talent. Donnie is most assuredly one of the finest guitar players you will ever hear.

Chris Golden: Son of William Lee Golden, Chris is a great producer and singer in his own right, and a terrific piano and mandolin player. In previous years he was the lead singer for the Goldens (mentioned in another chapter) and his voice has been heard on many big hit records.

Chris is the "Big Guy" on drums and provides a constant and consistent anchor for the Boys and band. He has been playing drums for us for seven years; however, he pretty much grew up on the Oaks' bus!

Jimmy Fulbright: A multi-talented and good-looking young man who plays bass guitar with an amazing flair and feel. The boy can also evermore sing! Jimmy excels on quite a few other instruments, as well, which adds to his versatility. He is a crowd favorite and we are honored to have him on our stage. He *is* the "Carolina Panther!"

Ryan Pierce: Ryan joined the MOB in August of 2003. He plays fiddle, steel guitar, and mandolin with an incredible youthful energy and style. He has added a lot of pure talent, musicianship, and energy to our stage. Ryan is a very positive young man who really cares about the music and his contributions over the past year have injected new life into every song we play!

Okay . . . a Little Math!

If you add up the 29 years of management by Jim Halsey, as well as the total years served by the Boys themselves, then add in the total of years put into this organization by all of the current employees of Oak Ridge Boys, Incorporated, you will come up with an astounding total of approximately 491 years.

That pretty well sums up our great organization and perhaps explains, once again, a few more reasons why the Oak Ridge Boys still exist and are able to perform at such a high level of professionalism!

Ron Fairchild

The Journey*
(Gospel mountain bluegrass)
Words and music by Joe Bonsall

I stumbled down a long dark road
From sunlight I had strayed
The demons came and beckoned me
I was lost and so afraid
I felt that I was falling
I thought it was a dream
I called upon my Father
To come and rescue me

Oh Father, rescue me

A door just seemed to open
The darkness turned to light
The Lord appeared before me
He wore a robe of white
He spoke my name so softly
I felt such peace within
He gently wrapped me in His arms
And forgave me all my sins

He forgave me all my sins

Another door was opened
A vision came so clear
I was on a ship now sailing
My Lord was standing near
He pointed toward the distant shore

And whispered to my soul,
"Your journey now is o'er my child
Rejoice and welcome home"

Rejoice and welcome home

I saw my precious mother
She was waiting by the river
She smiled and waved and called my name
There were angels all around her
No sickness, pain or sorrow
No strife, no fear of war
No devil's lies, no children cry
All is peace forever more

There is peace for ever more

Oh brother, my dear brother
Your life could end today
Except a man be born again
He cannot see the way
For Jesus there is waiting
To lead us past the grave
And take us home to be with Him
When the final journey's made

When the final journey's made

(Let's go home)

THE JOURNEY

The Merriam-Webster dictionary defines "faith" as "an allegiance to duty or a person, fidelity to one's promises, sincerity of intentions, complete trust, and belief and trust in and loyalty to God."

As I thought about where our life's journey has taken us, the first thing that came to mind was the fact that faith, in and of itself is such a personal thing. It is faith, or quite frankly, the lack of it, that could illustrate the difference in how a single life is lived and what is accomplished on our very short journey on this earth . . . and beyond. As I wrote in the epilogue of my book *G.I. Joe and Lillie,* "the key word here is faith. Faith in God, faith in country, faith in each other."

Within the confines of that book, I was talking about my mother Lillie Bonsall, who was the most influential person in my life. However, the Oak Ridge Boys are very well defined by this quote as well. As a group, and as individual men, we possess a strong and unwavering faith in those things that matter the most. Family, flag, friendship, and most importantly, a firm faith and belief in our Heavenly Father.

To a man, it has been our constant and consistent faith in God that has helped us to persevere and succeed in life on and off the stage, and we give Him the honor, praise, and glory for every precious moment.

Duane Allen, William Golden, Richard Sterban, and myself, Joe Bonsall, have yet one more common thread in the tapestry. This thread is surely the most important one. At a certain point in each man's life, he has opened up his heart to God and His glory by accepting Jesus Christ as a very personal Savior. It is a life changing experience to put all of your faith in Him, and the comfort, joy, and peace that overcomes your heart and soul is enormous. the Oak Ridge Boys are all born again, Bible-believing Christians.

Because of Christ's death on the cross of Calvary and His glorious ascension from the grave, we now possess the gift of life abundant and a peace within us that flows like a gentle river. It is this childlike faith that opens up all of the doors to God's blessings through His only begotten Son.

In Him, we also have the promise of eternal life when the final journey here is over. My Bible says that heaven and earth will soon pass and only what we do here on this earth for Christ will last.

Someday, we will all gather again on the heavenly shore where we will be known as we are known. We will see Jesus himself and live in His light. We will be reunited with our loved ones and friends who have gone before.

Can you just imagine what kind of singing there will be on that day? Power harmony for certain. It is pure faith that buys a ticket to that show. I hope to see you there.

– Joseph S. Bonsall

ALBUM DISCOGRAPHY

Gold, Platinum, Double Platinum

Over 20 Million Records Sold!

Y'all Come Back Saloon * . . . . September, 1977	Heartbeat . . . . September, 1987
Room Service * . . . . May, 1978	Monongahela . . . . August, 1988
Oak Ridge Boys Have Arrived * . . . . . . March, 1979	Greatest Hits Volume Three . . . . May, 1989
Together * . . . . March, 1980	American Dreams . . . . September, 1989
Greatest Hits ** . . . . October, 1980	Unstoppable . . . . April, 1991
Fancy Free *** . . . . May, 1981	Collection * . . . . April, 1992
Bobbie Sue * . . . . February, 1982	The Long Haul . . . . June, 1992
Oak Ridge Boys Christmas * . . . . . . September, 1982	Country Christmas Eve . . . . November, 1995
American Made * . . . . January, 1983	Revival . . . . March, 1997
Greatest Hits Two ** . . . . July, 1984	Voices . . . . July, 1999
Deliver * . . . . October, 1984	Millennium . . . . August, 2000
Step on Out . . . . March, 1985	From the Heart . . . . May, 2001
Seasons . . . . March, 1986	An Inconvenient Christmas . . . . September, 2002
Christmas Again . . . . September, 1986	Colors . . . . May, 2003
Where the Fast Lane Ends . . . . February, 1987	The Journey . . . . July, 2004

*Indicates gold **Indicates platinum ***Indicates double platinum

AWARDS

Listed by category in
chronological order

COUNTRY

ACADEMY OF COUNTRY MUSIC AWARDS
Best Vocal Group, 1977
Best Vocal Group, 1979
Best Album (*Y'all Come Back Saloon*), 1979
Single of the Year ("Elvira"), 1982

AMERICAN MUSIC AWARDS
Country Group of the Year, 1982
Best Country Music Video (*Everyday*), 1981

BOY SCOUTS OF AMERICA
Silver Buffalo Award, 2001

COUNTRY MUSIC ASSOCIATION AWARDS
Vocal Group of the Year, 1978
Instrumental Group of the Year
   (Oaks Band), 1978
Single of the Year ("Elvira"), 1981
Instrumental Group of the Year
   (Oaks Band), 1986

GRAMMY AWARDS
Best Vocal Performance by a Country
   Group or Duo ("Elvira"), 1982

MUSIC CITY NEWS FAN AWARDS
Band of the Year (Oaks Band), 1978
Best Single of the Year ("Elvira"), 1982

TNN VIEWERS CHOICE AWARDS
Favorite Group, 1988
Favorite Group, 1989

AMERICAN GUILD OF VARIETY ARTISTS
Best Country Vocal Group of the Year, 1981

BILLBOARD
Breakthrough Award, 1977
Number One Country Group, 1980
Number One Country Group/Singles, 1980
Number One Country Group/Albums, 1980
Bill Williams Memorial Award, 1981

BROADCAST MUSIC INC. (BMI)
Most Performed Song of the Year
   ("Elvira"), 1981

CASHBOX
Country Vocal Group/Singles, 1978
Country Vocal Group/Singles, 1979
Country Vocal Group/Albums, 1979
Country Vocal Group/Singles, 1980
Country Vocal Group/Albums, 1981
Country Crossover Group Pop/Singles, 1981
Country Crossover Group Pop/Albums, 1981
Country Crossover Group Pop/Singles, 1983

DISC JOCKEY AWARDS
Group of the Year/Country, 1980

INTERNATIONAL FAN CLUB ORGANIZATION
Tex Ritter Award, 1993

JUKE BOX OPERATORS OF AMERICA
Country Group of the Year, 1980
Song of the Year ("Elvira"), 1981

NATIONAL ASSOCIATION FOR CAMPUS ACTIVITIES
Best Major Country Performance, 1983
Best Major Country Performance, 1985
Best Major Country Performance, 1986

NATIONAL MUSIC COUNCIL
American Eagle Award, 1997

PERFORMANCE MAGAZINE READERS POLL
Country Act of the Year, 1981

RADIO & RECORDS COUNTRY MUSIC POLL
Country Group of the Year, 1978-1980
Single of the Year ("Elvira"), 1981

RADIO PROGRAMMERS CHOICE AWARDS
Vocal Group of the Year, 1981

RECORD WORLD
Country Singles Award, 1977
Country Vocal Group/Singles, 1978
Country Vocal Group/Albums, 1978
Country Vocal Group/Singles, 1980
Country Vocal Group/Albums, 1980
Country Vocal Group/Albums, 1981
Most Promising Male Group/Albums, 1981
Top Country Crossover Group, 1981

VOCAL GROUP HALL OF FAME
Inducted, September 2001

GOSPEL

DOVE AWARDS
Album of the Year, 1969
Album Jacket Design, 1969
Male Group of the Year, 1970
Album of the Year, 1972
Male Group of the Year, 1972
Album of the Year, 1973
Country Album of the Year, 2002

GOSPEL MUSIC HALL OF FAME
Inducted October, 2000

GRAMMY AWARDS
Best Vocal Performance by a Group or Duo/
   Gospel, 1971-1979 (four awards)

INTERNATIONAL

BILLBOARD/WEMBLEY FESTIVAL OF COUNTRY MUSIC
Best Country Group, 1975

COUNTRY RHYTHMS INTERNATIONAL FAN AWARDS
Best Country Group, 1982

KOUNTRY KORRAL MAGAZINE, SWEDEN
Number One Country Group, 1975
Number One Gospel Group, 1975

F.I.D.O.F (International Music Festival Organization)
Award of Excellence, 2003

PHOTO CREDITS

142

Courtesy of Duane Allen: 128

Dana Anderson / Allen Photo / Las Vegas, NV: 40

Brenda S. Ayres / Ayres Images / Houston, TX: 122

Cindy Barbush: 10

Kristin Barlowe: 11

Mindy Benson: 33

Courtesy of Joe Bonsall: 7, 32, 143

Mike Borum: 38

Watt Casey Jr.: 61, 75

Sonya Cogan / Courtesy of Jim Halsey: 37

Corbis: 47

Faye Dumph: 93

Sam Emerson: 140

Sherrie Evans: 23

Courtesy of Feed the Children: 99

Photograph by Jim Frey / Courtesy of Gaylord Program Services, Inc.: 57

Kathy Gangwisch: 29, 44, 51, 55, 56, 58, 59, 64, 65, 69, 78, 79, 82, 104, 106, 122

Photograph Courtesy of Gaylord Program Services, Inc.: 63

Libba Gillum / *Country Weekly* / Courtesy of Jim Halsey: 45

Courtesy of William Lee Golden: 100, 108, 120

Michael Gomez: 5, 8, 13, 18

Kathy Harris: 140, 141

David Johnson: Front Cover, Back Cover (left)

LeeAnn Lallone: 82, 122

Annie Leibovitz: 95

M. Alan Loveless Photography: 143

Alan L. Mayor: 25, 27, 88, 98, 129, 141

Alan Messer / www.alanmesser.com: 9, 12, 30, 31, 32, 34, 35, 41, 42, 43, 49, 54, 62, 67, 72, 80, 83, 85, 89, 90, 100, 101, 122, 129, Back Cover (top)

Jon Mir: 12, 15, 16, 17, 18, 19, 20, 22, 23, 32, 33, 35, 42, 53, 86, 87, 92, 99, 103, 110, 111, 112, 113, 114, 115, 116, 117, 119, 120, 121, 122, 124, 125, 126, 127, 128, 131, 132, 133, 134, 135, 136, 137, 138, 143

Jimmy Moore: 28, 39, 61, 78, 88, 97, 128, Back Cover (right center)

Marc Morrison: 73, 88, 123, 142

Courtesy of NRA: 101

Album Cover Courtesy of Oak Ridge Boys, Inc.: 66, 80

Artwork Courtesy of Oak Ridge Boys, Inc.: 21

Courtesy of Oak Ridge Boys, Inc.: 26

Jim Payton: 77

Chip Powell: 91

Don Putnam: 74, 96

Reflections Photo Inc: 110

Merry Ribnikar: 32

Billy Smith: 143

Donna Sterban: 13, 105, 107, 109, 126

Courtesy of Richard Sterban: 12

Joe Sugarman: 50

Michael Sykes: 129

Mark Tucker: 81

Raul Vega: 70

Richard Young: 40, 60

Chris Zar: 106

DEDICATION

Norah Lee Allen with Duane

You might have noticed that this book is dedicated to our wives, Mary Ann Bonsall, Norah Lee Allen, Brenda Golden, and Donna Sterban.

That is because without their love and commitment we would *not* exist. They have sacrificed more for the cause of this group than any other. We sing for you. We live for them!

So, for Mary Ann, Norah Lee, Brenda, and Donna:

There are too many nights spent alone without each other to caress and hold! A dark motel room, a long bus ride, a stage far away. There is an empty spot in your bed where my body should be, and I miss you. I love you more than life itself and there are times when the sacrifice is hard to bear. But I must sing, for it is what I was put here to do. Thank you for allowing me to follow my heart. Thank you for being there for me. Thank you for loving me!

It would seem that we are at full sail, my love, with a good sea and a strong wind. So light up the candles and gather up the children. Our course is set.

Tonight, we are coming home!

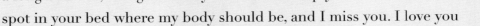

Donna Sterban

143

Mary Ann Bonsall with Sally Ann

Brenda Golden with William Lee and their son Solomon